smile
for life

A guide to overcoming your
fear of the dentist

DR. JAMES K. BAHCALL

ISBN: 1-929774-29-X

Library of Congress Control Number: 2003115926

Cover and Layout by Francine Smith
Illustrations by Clay Butler
Editing by Denaya J. Clark

This book is intended as a reference and guide for the
general public concerning oral healthcare. This book is not
a substitute for periodic check ups with health care professionals. The book is sold with the understanding that
neither the author nor publisher is engaged in providing
professional health care, service, or advice to any individuals.

6 17.6

Submit all requests for reprinting to:
Greenleaf Book Group LLC
8227 Washington Street, Suite #2,
Chagrin Falls, OH 44023
(440) 543-9300

Published in the United States by
Greenleaf Book Group LLC
Cleveland, Ohio.

www.greenleafbookgroup.com

ACKNOWLEDGMENTS

Although a manuscript may begin with a single idea from one individual, it is the dedication and hard work of many people that nurtures this single idea into book form.

I would like to express my sincere thanks to my editor, Virginia McCullough, who believed in this book from the very beginning and worked diligently to make it a reality. Also, I am indebted to Clint Greenleaf of Greenleaf Book Group, who provided the wings for this project to soar. I want to thank my publicist, Brian Feinblum and the entire staff at Planned Television Arts, and attorney, Charles Valente. Heartfelt thanks to my colleague and friend, Dr. Gerry Bradley, who provided invaluable critique and insight to the manuscript.

The support, love and encouragement from my family, Dr. Joseph and Barbara Himes, Albert and Esther Varon and Al and Joanne Bahcall have been a continued source of inspiration throughout my professional career.

To all my past and present students who taught me that it is not necessarily what you teach, but what you learn that counts, thank you for allowing me to be a part of your educational process.

In my academic career, I consider myself very lucky to have been surrounded by professors and deans who have enriched my mind with their vast knowledge and experience. Thank you for being mentors, colleagues and friends.

In closing, I would like to thank my wife, Amy, and children, Allie and Jamie, to whom I have dedicated this book for your unconditional love.

To my loving wife, Amy, and my adoring children, Allie and Jamie, for allowing me to reach for the stars everyday and still come home for dinner.

CONTENTS

It is what we know that prevents us from learning more.

– Albert Einstein

PREFACE

You may have noticed that TV producers have never made a show based on a dentist or an accountant. I suppose the day-to-day drama of dentists and accountants seems dull when compared to the image of trial attorneys fighting for justice in a courtroom or surgeons saving lives, all inside 60 minutes of primetime. Perhaps accountants feel slighted by being ignored, but I will go out on a limb (only a few inches) and boldly speak for all dentists everywhere when I say that based on the way Hollywood usually portrays our profession, we have enough trouble with image as it is. We don't need sitcoms to make it even worse.

Over the years, Hollywood producers have reinforced the dentist as a cause of fear and pain. Remember *Little Shop of Horrors*, *The Dentist*, and *Compromising Position*? They portrayed the dental profession in such a way that reinforced the image of the dental office as a mini-torture chamber and of dentists as "not quite normal." With an image like that, it's no wonder so many millions of people dread dental appointments or even worse, are extremely afraid to go to the dentist and may neglect their oral health because of it. Unfortunately, this fear persists, even in the face of enormous and important advances in dental treatment that have all but eliminated the discomfort and pain once associated with the drills and pliers and other horrific tools of the dentist's trade.

It's amazing to me that people go through major medical procedures like cardiac bypass surgery or organ transplants, but anticipating a trip to the dentist raises fear that doesn't compare with these medical experiences. Women have told me they would rather give birth than seek dental treatment! I knew the image of dentistry had hit bottom when my own mother joined the chorus describing dentists as "purveyors of pain."

My mother voiced her opinion when, after a few years of practicing general dentistry, I decided to enter specialty training in endodontics (root canal treatment). About fifty-four endodontic programs exist in the United States, the majority of which are university-based. (The other programs are located in hospitals, primarily Veteran's Administration hospitals.) About three or four resident positions per program are available each year, which results in fierce competition among the 75-200 annual applicants to every program.

I clearly recall receiving my acceptance letter to the postgraduate endodontic program at Marquette University School of Dentistry. I was filled with excitement about expanding my professional horizons, but a few concerns about selling my general practice also led to some sleepless nights.

However, what stands out is the day I had lunch with my mother. My plan was to wait until dessert was served to surprise her with my great news, but I was so excited about my acceptance to the endodontic program that I thought I might burst. I just couldn't wait to tell her, so I blurted out the news before we even ordered our lunch. I remember her response so clearly it might have happened yesterday. First, she winced, as if she'd bit her tongue. Then she said, "Why would you want to go into a field that hurts people?"

I almost dropped my water glass. But then I patiently proceeded to explain the value and virtue of root canal treatment. My "lecture" got me nowhere. I couldn't convince my own mother that learning to perform root canals to save my patients' teeth was a noble pursuit.

Now, I know my mother loves me and supports me with all the fervor of most devoted mothers, so I understood that her stubborn attitude wasn't a personal attack, but rather a social statement on the bad image of root canal treatment. I was sure that my mother's thinking was no different than thousands-even millions-of other Americans. Would she have said the same thing if I'd said I'd decided to become a cardiac surgeon or a physical therapist? Probably not. The worst association of treatment and pain seems to be reserved for dentists.

The negative image of dentists probably has its

"roots" in the era of the Wild West. Back then, the dentist wore many hats. It was not uncommon for a dentist to be a blacksmith, barber, and tooth puller! The choice of anesthetic was a shot of whiskey or moonshine. I should note that during a tooth extraction, both the patient and the dentist took this local anesthetic. The shot of alcohol helped the dentist calm his nerves while the patient screamed bloody murder during the dental procedure. Thank goodness the field of dentistry has come a long way from these humble beginnings, even if the image hasn't.

Why You Should Keep Reading

All branches of oral healthcare form a small but strong supporting spoke in the overall wheel of healthcare. In the big picture, your oral health can't be separated from the condition of the rest of your body. This seems to be big news to many people, but it isn't news to dentists and physicians.

The condition of your teeth may have a direct effect on your ability to properly digest food. Your digestive tract doesn't begin in your stomach; it starts in your mouth with your teeth. Optimal digestion depends on normal ability to chew your food. (Slowing down long enough to chew is a factor, too.) Last, but not least, the cause of what you label a "tension headache" may be malocclusion, that is, an abnormal bite. In addition, the appearance of one's teeth can have a great impact on self-confidence. Cosmetic dentistry treatment involves repairing broken or chipped teeth and using tooth-whitening procedures that give a patient the same personal aesthetic appeal as any plastic surgery procedure designed to "hide" the signs of aging.

A range of relatively inexpensive procedures is available to restore "dental self-esteem." So, it's no exaggeration to say that your dentist is one of your most important healthcare providers. If you don't have one, then use the information in this book to go find one-now! If you happen to be one of the 30-40 million adults who does not seek regular dental care, then I hope this book will allay your fears. In fact, I include specific chapters that address the "dental phobic."

This book has a mission, and that is to help the general public fully understand today's dentistry, with all its sophisticated treatment and important aesthetic component. Consider it a handy guide to modern dental care for the whole family.

"Speaking of family," today's kids do not have the same fear of the dentist that is still common among adults. This is due in part to the fact that children have fewer cavities because of better early preventative treatment. In addition, many children see pediatric dentists who are trained in patient management skills, which in turn set the stage in a child's mind to understand that oral health care is something to be valued. The person who "delivers" this preventive care can be looked at as a friendly adult, rather than a feared authority figure who puts kids in big chairs and then makes their lives miserable for twenty minutes.

Not Your Grandparents' Dentists

Recent decades have brought enormous advances in healthcare and significant changes in the way we treat common conditions and diseases. The same is true for dentistry, although you may not hear much about these advances. Where clacking dentures were once part of "old age" jokes, today the goal is to keep the teeth we had as kids. Adult orthodontics and other smile-improving measures are common in dental practice. As you'll see, dentists are seldom just plain ol' dentists anymore. There are specialists for every stage of dental care throughout your life.

The Heart Bone is Connected to the Tooth Bone

Many people, including but certainly not limited to dental phobics, think that the mouth has no relationship to the rest of the body. The same people who take meticulous care of their skin, for example, lack good oral hygiene because "teeth are *just* teeth," not an eye or a leg.

This "just teeth" attitude might go back to the fact that dentists of years past were trained like "tooth mechanics." Times have changed. Today's dental training incorporates many of the same courses that medical students take as part of their curriculum. Dental students are educated about the relationship of the oral cavity to the rest of the body. This education continues when a dentist goes on to a dental residency, specialty training, or continuing education courses. *Oral physicians* have replaced the tooth mechanic professional.

Dentists who practice as oral physicians take thorough medical and dental patient histories, check blood pressure, and perform an extensive oral examination. This is done before any other dental treatment is rendered.

Twenty-first century dentists are often the first health care professionals to pick up a patient's hypertension (high blood pressure). As you may know, hypertension is a "silent disease," meaning that it produces no symptoms. People can walk around with high blood pressure without being aware of it. For many individuals, a trip to the dentist is relatively routine (because they've taken the "twice a year check-up" recommendations seriously). Therefore, they're more likely to see a dentist before they see a physician. Since so many of today's dentists take patients' blood pressure, the first indication of hypertension may occur in the dentist's chair.

Based on a patient's medical history, the dentist often contacts the primary care physician to discuss any health concerns that may contraindicate a dental treatment procedure. One systemic problem not wide-ly known is the connection between heart disease and the condition of the teeth.

As an endodontist (a specialist in root canal treatment), I have seen my share of patients in pain. But sometimes the tooth may not be the cause of toothache pain. A few years ago, a man in his mid-60s was referred to me from his general dentist. He reported no medical problems and his chief com-plaint was pain around his lower left canine tooth. The patient described the pain as a common toothache, but when I examined the teeth in that area, they tested within normal limits. At that point, I asked him about the onset of his pain. The man said he noticed it when he walked up stairs. I then asked if he ever felt pain in his chest or had difficul-ty breathing after climbing the stairs. He said that he had no pain in his chest to speak of, but he would feel a little winded, which he thought was due to the physical activity of climbing the stairs. As you may know, about 10 percent of patients with heart disease have pain referred to the jaw region, usually in the front part of the lower jaw. Most people dismiss this because they have been educated that heart attacks cause severe pain in the chest that can radiate down the left arm.

I explained the lack of dental findings and then referred this patient to a cardiologist his internist had recommended. In fact, I insisted that he see the cardiologist that same day and I had my office staff call and schedule him for an appointment. Before the end of office hours, the cardiologist called and said that my patient had blockage in his coronary arteries and that he was scheduled for bypass surgery first thing in the morning. Fortunately, the story has a happy ending: This gentleman recovered from the heart surgery with out complication and continues to live a full and active life.

This story is not intended to increase anxiety among those who already avoid dental care. My desire is to educate individuals about the importance of oral health care and its relationship to the rest of the body. I also want you to fully understand the scope of today's dentistry. I designed this book to help you understand all the available choices and possibilities as you tend to your oral health in the twenty-first century. But I also hope that the information will be a catalyst to change the way the general public views dentists and dentistry. Since whiskey and pliers are a thing of the past, who knows? One day we might see a TV series based on the life of a dentist.

Chapter One

• • •

SORRY, I DON'T SPEAK THE LANGUAGE

"Dentist" is the familiar title, but as you probably know, it encompasses many things, including a list of specialties ending in "ist." We become dentists and one or more of the "ists" through specialized training. At least part of feeling comfortable when you see a dentist is gaining an understanding about how he or she gained the necessary knowledge and skills to "put out a shingle" and practice.

Strange as it seems, it wasn't very long ago when all a person had to do to become a dentist was either go to barber school or become an apprentice of another practicing dentist. Way back when, as long as a dentist had a dental chair, whiskey for anesthetic, and a hitching post for a patient's horse, he (and at one time they were almost exclusively male) was granted a state license.

Today, dentistry is a full-fledged healthcare science and a pre-dental, four-year undergraduate education includes extensive math and science courses. Over 95 percent of students entering dental school have a B.S. or B.A. degree. Dental schools look for a high grade point average, along with a good score on the standard admission test called the DAT (Dental School Admissions Test).

Except for the University of the Pacific, which is a 3-year program, dental school is an additional four years of demanding education. In contrast with medical school, a dental student is the primary physician of their patients' comprehensive care starting in their second or third year of dental school. Comprehensive care means the totality of treatment and management of a person's oral health. Although a medical student sees patients in their third and fourth years and participates in short clinical patient rotations (i.e. 8 weeks surgery, 8 weeks internal medicine, etc.), comprehensive patient care for an M.D. starts during a medical student's internship and residency. In addition to the course work and clinical requirements for graduation, a dental student must successfully pass a written national board examination.

I went to school at Tufts University School of Dental Medicine in Boston, Massachusetts, and after completing the four years of study, I earned the degree DMD (Doctor of Dental Medicine). The other designation is DDS (Doctor of Dental Surgery). The degrees are exactly the same, and which degree is given depends only on the university's tradition.

After graduation, dentists must pass a state board examination (usually given as a multi-state exam) before being able to practice. The exam involves both written and clinical sections, which as implied, involves the clinical examination of patients. Graduation from dental school is very exciting, but the board exam can be nerve-racking. I, for one, was very cool under all those beads of sweat on my forehead when I sat for my state-licensing exam.

After successfully passing the state board examination, a brand spanking new dentist can go into private practice, the military, or complete a one-year general practice residency in a hospital or a one-year advanced general dentistry program in a dental college. Alternatively, new dentists can also continue their education by specializing in one of the nine dental specialties recognized by the American Dental Association (ADA). This usually means another two- to four-year program at a dental school or hospital.

The ADA is the professional association of dentists, and as such it has a mission to remain committed to the general public's oral health. It regulates the ethical principles and behavior within the profession; and better than one dentist could do alone, the ADA monitors science and professional advancement and initiatives in advocacy, education, research, and the development of standards. This is a fancy way of saying that the organization educates both the public and its own members, and it advocates for high standards in education and practice. The ADA has been around a while; it was in 1859, in

Niagara Falls, New York, by 26 dentists representing various dental societies in the United States. Today, the ADA has more than 141,000 members.

In addition to general practice, the ADA formally recognizes the following nine specialty areas of dental practice:

1. ***Dental Public Health:*** A dentist who specializes in controlling dental diseases and promoting dental health through organized community efforts. These dental specialists are usually based at a dental school. Their main concern is dental health education of the public and prevention of dental disease on a community basis.

2. ***Endodontist:*** A dentist who specializes in root canal treatment.

3. ***Oral and Maxiofacial Pathology:*** The specialist that deals with the identification and treatment of diseases affecting the oral and maxillofacial area (this encompasses the mouth and the face below the eye region.) These specialists are usually based at a dental school. They help identify cancer and other non-cancer type lesions of the oral cavity through clinical, biopsy, or x-ray examination.

4. ***Oral and Maxillofacial Radiology:*** The specialty within dentistry that uses x-ray technology to help diagnosis dental disease. Usually based in dental schools, these specialists function much like a radiologist in a hospital.

5. ***Oral and Maxillofacial Surgeon:*** A dentist who specializes in extracting teeth and performing various types of jaw surgery. These are the dental specialists who remove wisdom teeth and perform more advance types of surgical procedures in the mouth (i.e. removal of pathology (diseased tissue) and repositioning jaws for better esthetics and oral function).

6. ***Orthodontist:*** A dentist who specializes in straightening teeth with braces.

7. ***Pediatric Dentist:*** A dentist who specializes in treating kids.

8. ***Periodontist:*** A dentist who specializes in treating gum disease.

9. ***Prosthodontist:*** A dentist who specializes in placing crowns, bridges, and dentures.

The general dentist can practice all these different specialties under the guidelines of their particular state licensure. However, it is quite common for a dentist to refer a patient to a dental specialist for a second opinion or for particular treatment. The general dentist operates like the gatekeeper. Unlike the situation in medicine today, where a patient may call a dermatologist (skin doctor) or an ophthalmologist (eye doctor) without seeing a family physician first, individuals usually see a general dentist first before a referral to a specialist is made. (I am speaking here in generalities, rather than what a particular insurance plan may dictate.)

When general dentists refer patient to specialists, it doesn't mean these dentists are incompetent. Rather, it should make patients more confident in their dentists because they are not cavalier about treatments they do not perform routinely. In fact, licensed dentists are able to perform any dental procedure. However, the dental specialties provide an avenue for referral to those who have shown a particular interest in developing skills in one of the many areas of dental healthcare.

Chapter Two

• • •

AVOIDING THE ROAD TO BAD ORAL HEALTH

Dental disease and pain can be compared to the domino effect, which in this case, has nothing to do with either pizza chains or international relations. But it does concern what happens when individuals with a simple cavity ignore the symptoms. They might ignore twinges in a tooth for all kinds of reasons, including their fear of going to a dentist, the fact that they're short of money, or they hope if they ignore a problem it will go away. However, pain anywhere in the body is a signal that something is amiss, and pretending the discomfort doesn't exist is a sure road to more serious problems.

The people who ignore dental pain fall into two general categories: *procrastinators* and the *phobics*. While someone who has a phobia in the true psychological sense may need help to overcome the problem, procrastinators can wait too long to seek help, too, and often end up turning a little problem into a big one.

The Road Looks Something Like This...

You take a big gulp of an iced drink or roll some ice cream around in your mouth, and then, ouch! But you ignore it as an *anomaly*, if you like "scientific" words, and if you don't, you call it a "nothing serious incident." But then the tooth continues to become sensitive to cold, and soon, hot tea or coffee sets off the twinge, too. In order to avoid that twinge, you may begin watching the temperature of your food and beverages, thus also avoiding the dentist. A few weeks or months later the pain seems to miraculously go away. However, temperature sensitivity in teeth is usually caused by a cavity irritating the nerve of a tooth.

I've heard about a few home remedies for toothaches, including the one that recommends keeping the tooth bathed in whisky. Apparently, this was passed down through the generations. Those who like this approach tell themselves that it was worth putting up with the pain, because they saved themselves a trip to the dentist and were able to consume a lot of whiskey. They go on with the ups and downs of everyday life without a dreaded toothache.

Regardless of the way you avoid the toothache— or why—a few months later you may wake up to swelling in your gums or your face and possible pain during *mastication*, which is more scientific jargon for chewing food. A strange twist on the path happens now. The procrastinators go into full swing. If they were "too busy" to go to the dentist they suddenly find the time. Many of those who didn't have the cash suddenly discover some.

But, if you have a genuine fear of going to a dentist, then you deal with the pain for another few months. However, sooner or later, if you ignore the problem you may have nearly constant pain and your tooth becomes slightly loose. (Or is that your imagination?) Finally, a few more months go by and the tooth in question is *significantly* looser.

If you are a procrastinator and still have delayed addressing the problem, then at this point you may give in and begin asking around about dentists. Frankly, at this point, the best dentist is the one who can take you immediately. For many people the delaying tactics stop here. In fact, those who thought they didn't have the time or money begin kicking themselves (figuratively speaking!) for not handling the problem sooner.

On the other hand, true dental phobics may also talk themselves into finding a dentist. They also ask around and get a phone number from a friend. Then they stare at the dentist's phone number for weeks. During this time, they may occasionally pick up the phone in an attempt to call the dentist, but they quickly hang up after punching a few numbers on the phone. I talked with one person who became bold enough to dial all the numbers and listened long enough for the receptionist to answer, but then he quickly hung up. This person even said he was afraid the dental office had caller ID and he was sure the receptionist would call back and try to corner him into to scheduling an appointment. In my experience, it could take a year or more before the person with a true dental phobia arrives at the dentist office, usually with the appointment card in his shaking hands and beads of perspiration forming on his forehead.

This is What I Get For Waiting

When our true dental phobics and some very serious procrastinators finally agree to sit in the dental chair, the dentist performs a thorough examination and takes a few x-rays of the tooth in question. The dentist may then explain how the simple cavity became larger, then infiltrated the nerve, which then became inflamed, and was the cause of the sensitivity to cold and hot temperatures. Over time, the nerve in the tooth died. This happened because by nature, a tooth has a limited amount of healing ability. The death of the nerve roughly coincides with the point at which the patient thought the home remedy worked because the pain went away. But this is an illusion. What really happens is that an infection develops that spreads around the tooth and causes the fibers that hold the tooth to the bone to become irritated, hence pain on chewing.

The body's immune system reacts by removing the infection, but also removing the bone that helps the tooth stay firm in the socket. The body defends against bacteria or foreign matter by triggering certain cells to fight against these invaders. The cells that help to remove the infection cannot differentiate between the bacteria and the bone that supports the tooth. Thus, the bone is removed during this invasion. Clinical signs may appear, including the tooth becoming loose because of loss of supporting bone tissue. The area around the tooth appears *radiolucent* on the x-ray, meaning that since there is less bone in the area, more x-ray beams are able to hit the film, causing the x-ray film to be darker.

It is difficult to regenerate bone, and the only viable treatment option is to take the tooth out. If it is a back tooth, the space that remains from the tooth extraction will make it difficult to chew. If it happens to be a front tooth that needs extraction, then both eating and cosmetic concerns arise.

If the person agrees to complete treatment, then the dentist will recommend replacing the tooth with a bridge that incorporates the two adjacent teeth or with an implant, which is a metal post-like object that is placed in the extraction site. Then a crown is placed over it. Both these treatment options are effective and long-lasting, and they certainly resolve the effects of the missing tooth. However, these treatments are expensive and involve multiple visits to the dentist, which is bad news for the dental phobic.

Stopping the Domino Effect

The faster a patient prevents or stops the domino effect of dental disease, problems can be resolved with less treatment and fewer trips to the dentist. In general, fear of the dentist is greatly reduced among those who see their dentist regularly. In fact, if you see your dentist every six months for a check-up and cleaning, the chances of a cavity even forming are slim. Just to be clear, the reason for the six-month period is not some master plan of the ADA to make money for dentists. This timeframe is based on scientific studies that have shown that this is the average time it takes for decay to invade a tooth.

Dental Phobia is Not a Joke

I try to take a light approach when comparing dental procrastinators with dental phobics. But in actuality, it isn't really a light problem, and given today's advanced dental technology and options, it should be a phenomenon of the past. Dental phobia should go the way of pliers and whiskey in the dental practice, but alas, the condition remains a fact of life.

If you're a procrastinator, you can change your ways and I hope this book helps you; but if you're a dental phobic, don't give up hope. Understanding the advances in dentistry and finding an understanding dentist will help you overcome the problem.

Anxiety and Fear and Phobia...Oh My!

Some definitions to keep in mind:

- *Anxiety:* A reaction to the unknown.
- *Fear:* A reaction to a known danger.
- *Phobia:* A marked and persistent fear that reaches the extent that the individual entirely avoids the situation.
- *Oh My!:* It has been estimated 30-40 million people in the U.S. do not seek dental treatment on a regular basis or totally avoid it due to either anxiety, fear, and/or phobia of going to the dentist.

As you can see, many millions of individuals still have at least some degree of fear of dental treatment. If you are one of them, I hope the information in this book will reassure you that it's a new day in dentistry, and your fear is keeping you from enjoying the oral health you deserve.

Chapter Three

• • •

FIGHTING THE CAVITY CREEPS

You're undoubtedly familiar with the term *cavity*, which is what most people dread when they go to the dentist. The dental jargon for a cavity is *caries*. Treating a cavity is one of the most common procedures performed in dentistry. We seldom think of a cavity as a medical "ailment," but like the common cold and back pain, dental caries is one of the most common human health complaints. A high percentage of the adult population in the U.S. has some form of silver in their teeth, which was put there to fill a cavity. I myself have enough silver in my mouth to be a receptor for satellite radio.

Bad experiences with cavity treatment procedures of the past form the reason many dental phobics stopped seeking dental care, and these bad dental visits contribute to procrastination and anxiety among the relatively "normal." I have talked with many men and women who had a horrific experience in the dental chair while seeking what is standard treatment for a routine oral health concern. The bad dental experience might have been due to poor technology of the past, or perhaps the patient didn't understand what was involved in the procedure, or did not have a good rapport with the dentist. Stories about bad dental experiences spread quickly, and this can feed others' apprehension, in a reinforcing kind of way, in that individuals become fearful that this will happen to them if they "risk" going to the dentist.

Unfortunately, some of these bad dental experiences may have resulted from being treated by someone who was not up-to-date on current treatment or, frankly, was clinically incompetent. Fortunately, these scenarios are few and far between, but one cannot discount this factor in any profession. You must protect your own well-being, so if you find yourself in this situation, immediately seek a new dentist.

What is a Cavity Anyway?

The word "cavity" actually refers to dental decay that occurs when certain bacteria (about 300 types of oral bacteria exist) use the sugar from food we consume and transform it into energy. The bacterial by-product from this energy is acid, which erodes the enamel and will continue if not stopped until it gets to the nerve of the tooth (ouch!). (See Figure 1)

Many adults (especially the dental phobics) believe that only kids can get decay. But adults can not only get what is called secondary decay, which is

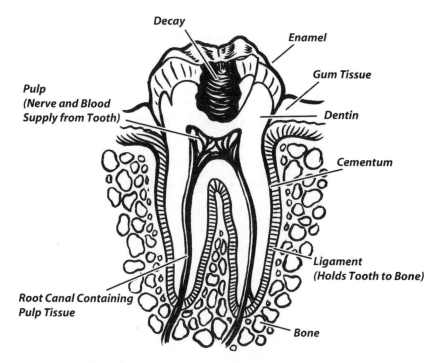

Tooth Anatomy and Decay – Figure 1.

decay that forms around a previous filling, but they can also develop decay in new areas on a tooth, generally on the side of the tooth. A related issue is gum disease that caused the gum line to recede or move down from the tooth, thereby exposing more of the dental root. The outer surface of the root is a hard tissue called *cementum*, which is like enamel, only softer. This means that the acid that forms from bacteria can penetrate the surface faster. This causes potential pain and discomfort.

How Do I Know if I Have a Cavity?

Dental decay is diagnosed by x-ray or by feeling the stickiness of the tooth decay with a dental instrument called an explorer. Currently, there is research and development of a new instrument that uses a fluorescent-type light to detect tooth decay before it is even visible on x-ray or by the touch of a dental explorer. When the light is placed over a tooth, it detects any loss of calcium and phosphate in the tooth's surface. It will also detect secondary caries and root cavities. By detecting decay early, the process can be reversed or stopped with minimal treatment.

If the decay is limited to the enamel only, in most cases it can be removed without anesthetic. However, if the decay is in the *dentin* (a softer mineralized tissue that is directly under enamel and cementum) or cementum the dentist will recommend some type of anesthesia, which helps you to be comfortable during the procedure.

The decay is usually removed with the dental drill or sometimes a laser. Lasers have been around for about 10 years in dentistry, and some dentists use the technology to remove decay that is not too deep in the tooth. If the decayed area is large, a dental drill is still the best method of removing the decay. After the decay is removed, the dentist will place a silver filling or a tooth-color filling called *composite* or resin into the tooth. The silver filling is *amalgam*, meaning it is a mixture of different metals, and the composite or resin is a type of plastic that hardens when a special light is illuminated on to its surface.

After the filling is placed, the dentist will have you bite down on a thin sheet of paper called *marking paper*. The paper "marks" if you are biting too hard on the new filling. We call it a "high spot," and if one is detected, it is adjusted until proper biting function is restored. This is usually the end of treatment for a single "episode" of dental caries.

The Truth About Dental Amalgam

In the last 10 or 15 years (and even longer in some circles), we've seen many media reports about dental amalgam. Unfortunately, sometimes media reports about healthcare issues can confuse the public rather than educate. Media reports have repeated claims that the mercury from the amalgam can cause certain systemic diseases such as Multiple Sclerosis (MS) or brain tumors. However, no scientific study has linked amalgam to these types of medical disorders. Dental amalgam has been used to restore teeth for over 100 years and the ADA maintains that it is safe for dental usage. Over the years, millions of amalgam fillings have been place and fewer than 100 cases of an allergic reaction to amalgam have *ever* been reported in the dental literature. These reactions were similar to a typical skin allergy.

Prevention is for Adults and Kids Alike

Preventing tooth decay is just as important for adults as it is for children, and while it isn't a particularly complex process, it does require practicing all those "virtues" we don't like to hear about: discipline, commitment, care, persistence. So, if you want to prevent the cavity creeps from invading your mouth, do the following:

- Limit sweets like candy and cake—the heavily sugared snack and dessert foods. Rinse your mouth with water or brush your teeth after eating sweets.
- Brush your teeth twice a day with toothpaste that contains fluoride.
- Floss your teeth a least once a day.
- Get dental checks-ups every six months.

Chapter Four

• • •

No Pain, but Much Gain

Someone once said that the power of the anticipation of an event is much greater than the actual event. This is certainly true when it comes to dental exams, particularly when a dental phobic first visits the dentist for an oral examination. In order to understand what happens during an exam, keep in mind a few simple ideas, one of which is that, for the sake of simplicity, permanent teeth are universally numbered from 1-32. Tooth #1 is the patient's upper right third molar and the numbers follow around the upper arch to tooth #16 which is the patient's upper left third molar. The lower left third molar is #17 and the numbers follow around to the patient's lower right third molar that represents tooth #32. (See Figure 2)

So, operating from the maxim that "knowledge is power," this is what happens during a dental exam:

- The dentist first looks into a patient's mouth to get a picture of the state of overall oral health.
- The teeth are examined to check for decay and to see how previous tooth restorations are holding up.
- The dentist then examines the gum tissue by

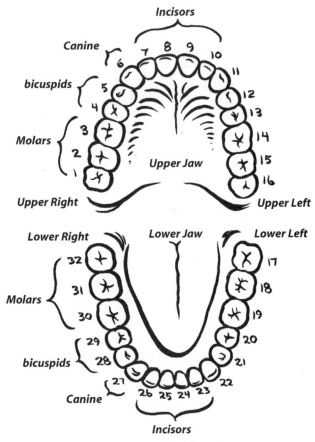

Permanent Teeth - Figure 2.

looking at the color and probing the tissue around each tooth to check for periodontal disease.
- After this preliminary exam, the dentist will then examine the tongue, cheek, lips, salivary, and lymph node glands and other soft tissue of the mouth.

If a patient has not had recent oral x-rays over the past 12 to 18 months, the dentist will usually take x-rays. If the dentist finds a cavity or a defective filling, for example, he or she may use a special intra-oral camera to take a picture of the tooth or teeth; the image is projected on a monitor. Patients can see the image on the monitor as the dentist explains any problem and suggests proper treatment to correct the problem. The dentist has the capability to print these images and place them into the patient's record for future reference.

As you can see, nothing is going to happen during this exam that will cause discomfort. You may feel slight pressure or a sting when the dentist uses a probe to examine a spot on the tooth or on the gum line. However, in general, it's safe to say that the dental exam is a pain-free procedure.

That "C" Word

Discussing cancer always arouses some discomfort, and while there have been advancements in cancer treatment, prevention is the first key, and early detection the second, which is where dentists play an important role. According to an article by Dr. Sol Silverman, published in the November, 2001 *Journal of the American Dental Association*, oral and throat cancers represent approximately three percent of all cancers in the United States. The problem is that by the time oral or throat cancers are usually detected, the long-term prognosis is not very good. Most oral cancers are not painful and dental phobia is so common that these cancers are often at a more advanced stage when diagnosed.

You can help *prevent* oral and throat cancer by not smoking (and quitting if you already are a smoker) and using sunscreen to protect your lips from the ultraviolet rays of the sun. In addition, the antioxidant vitamins A, C, and E have long been associated with overall cancer prevention.

Oral cancer screening is part of the twice-yearly dental exam. This involves reviewing medical and dental history and performing *extraoral* (outside of the mouth) and *intraoral* (inside the mouth) examinations. The tongue, the tissue inside of the cheek, gum tissue, and the throat area are viewed in the examination, and the dentist will palpate the lymph nodes in the submandibular (under the lower jaw) region and the neck. All this takes only a few minutes. This is an important exam because it represents early screening for problems associated with oral health. In addition, if this is a first visit, the thorough examination helps a patient begin to feel comfortable with the dentist.

If a dentist observes something on the tissue that *may* vary from the norm, he or she may take a biopsy (tissue sample), usually performed without anesthesia. A stiff-bristled brush removes some cells from the suspicious area and this biopsy sample is then sent to the lab for evaluation. Some dentists refer patients to an oral pathologist or oral surgeon for the biopsy and examination.

Do not be overly concerned if a biopsy is taken. This procedure is done for the same reasons a dermatologist removes suspicious skin lesions. Most of the time the biopsy report comes back negative, but you can be assured that the test was done to rule out cancer.

Should the biopsy report come back positive for cancer, the dentist usually refers the patient to an oncologist (a physician specializing in cancer treatment). The oncologist will work with a team of pathologists, radiologists, and head and neck surgeons to provide the best possible care for a patient. An auxiliary team of the patient's general dentist, nurses, speech pathologists, prosthodontists (dentists specializing in placing crowns, bridges, and dentures), and nutritionists may all be a part of oral cancer treatment plans.

Pretreatment for Some Patients

Some individuals have a systemic medical condition that could be affected by dental treatment. For example, a person with a history of certain types of a heart murmur may be instructed by their physician to take an antibiotic prior to treatment. The reason for this is that is that a murmur is a pathological or congenital defect in a heart valve, which is susceptible to infection or inflammation. It is possible that a dental procedure could release bacteria into the blood stream and cause an infection of the heart valve. This could put a patient at serious risk, therefore, the American Heart Association recommends that patients with a certain type of heart murmur or heart valve replacement be pre-medicated with an antibiotic. The standard antibiotic prescribed to a patient is Amoxicillin, 2gms one hour before any dental treatment. If the patient is allergic to Amoxicillin, then Clindamycin 600mg is prescribed one hour before dental treatment. "Yesterday's dentists" might have overlooked this medical condition and focused their attention only on detecting and treating tooth decay without any concern for the overall well-being of the patient. Today's dentists take a "whole patient" approach to dental care.

What a Pain in the Face

It is important for a patient to differentiate pain from a tooth (*odontogenic*) and pain from the head and face (*crainofacial*) region. Unfortunately, at times this is easier said than done. It is not uncommon for a patient to think a pain is coming from a tooth when in fact the source of the pain is of neural or muscular origin of the head or face. On the other hand, a tooth can be the source of facial or head pain.

Dentists can help you differentiate tooth pain

from pain originating in the head and face region. Symptoms usually *not* caused by tooth pain include burning, tingling or "electric-like" sensations. Dentists will examine your teeth in order to see if they can reproduce the pain. They may also use a diagnostic technique called "selective anesthesia," which means you are given local anesthesia around the tooth or teeth that is suspected of being the source of pain. If the anesthesia alleviates the pain then usually we can conclude that the pain originates in the tooth. If the pain persists, its source is usually crainofacial muscles and nerves, in which case you may be referred to a dental specialist (oral surgeon) or a physician for further evaluation.

Common non-odontogenic pain can be caused by the following:

1. ***TMJ (temporomandibular joint):*** the symptoms usually involve pain in the ear and muscles around the TMJ-the jaw joint.

2. ***Trigeminal Neuralgia:*** symptoms usually are a sharp pain sensation if your face is touched, even lightly. The pain subsides immediately after the pressure of the touch is removed. In other words, touching activates the pain; avoiding any touch to the face helps prevent the pain from beginning.

3. ***Cardiac origin:*** symptoms can radiate to the lower jaw, especially the lower left anterior (front) portion.

4. ***Maxillary sinus:*** symptoms are usually a feel-

ing of fullness in the face or tooth pain in the entire quadrant of the upper jaw.

As an endodontist, patients often are referred to me because they have pain that is difficult to diagnosis. When it comes to diagnosing pain in the mouth, I always look for horses and not zebras! This means that I look for the garden-variety sources, such as a nerve problem in a tooth or a tooth fracture, rather than some rare pathology. Over the years, I have seen cases in which the practitioner began looking for zebras right away and jumping to the conclusion that the pain was crainofacial in origin, when in fact it was a variety of horse; a cracked root on a tooth, for example.

It is important to communicate the type and duration of mouth pain you're experiencing. When it is difficult to localize pain that appears to be coming from the mouth, a dentist may prescribe anti-inflammatory medication or an antibiotic to help isolate the source of the pain. I sometimes even recommend that patients keep a journal for a few days to document when the pain is triggered. It could start when eating or perhaps it just wakes you up at night, seemingly out of the blue. The journal can help the dentist see patterns, which helps in making a diagnosis.

Chapter Five

• • •

THE BIG THREE OF
A DENTAL OFFICE VISIT

Dental offices offer their own "sensory experiences," some of which contribute to anxiety and fear. Even those who do not have an inordinate amount of apprehension when they visit the dentist still approach the office with a degree of resignation. Let's face it, a dental visit is a time to endure rather than enjoy. For most people, the experience begins the minute they open the door to the office and encounter the first of the "Big Three."

What's that Smell?

The sense of smell is powerful, and it is our most "emotional" sense because unlike the other senses, it is first processed in the emotional center of the brain, what we often call the "primitive" brain. Our sense of smell has a long emotional "memory" and often contributes to the pleasure of ordinary things like the scent of favorite flowers or appealing cooking smells wafting from the kitchen. Equally important, the smells associated with disturbing or traumatic events are remembered, too, like the acrid odor of smoke damage after a fire.

As poets and philosophers have observed over the centuries, the sense of smell has the ability to transport us to a different time. We may not remember what we did yesterday, but a certain smell can propel us back 20 years to a special or particularly meaningful event. The smell of the dental office may have the same effect on certain people. But unlike a special event of the past, the smell can bring back vivid memories of fear and pain experienced as a kid during dental visits, which may have occurred when the field of dentistry was not as advanced as it is today.

If dental office smells bother you or trigger a fear response, remember that as much as smells alter thought perception, by its nature, the way you experience a smell dissipates once the receptor sites in the nose are stimulated and the smell is processed. Think how often you walk in to a restaurant and the aromas immediately set your taste buds dancing. But after this initial sensation, the scents in the restaurant quickly become unnoticeable and soon, different smells stimulate your nose.

This principle holds true in a dental office. After you enter the office the initial smell will quickly become unnoticeable. I have to admit that the smell of the dental office was one of the factors that made me think about dentistry as a career. The smell may be a little sterile, but I have always correlated it with "clean and fresh," much the way I perceived the cleanliness of the dental instruments I would want placed into my mouth. If I walked into a dental office that had an odor of dirt and grime, I would never feel comfortable being treated there.

If you correlate the smell of a dental office with fear, try to put a positive spin on it. Think of the office as an extension of your home. Remember that someone has taken the necessary steps to make this a safe environment for you. All dental offices in the US must comply with OSHA (Occupational Safety and Health Administration) regulations. OSHA has federal guidelines that mandate a safe office environment for staff and patients. If a dentist does not comply with OSHA standards, he or she can be fined and the office be can closed down until these regulations are met.

Remember that the typical dental office smell exists because of the strict procedures that require all instruments to be sterilized at high temperatures after each patient use. In addition, the examining room that includes the dental chair, dental light, countertops, and so forth, are all wiped down with disinfectant solution after each patient.

These days, some dentists' offices are using aromatherapy in the form of scented candles or essential oils that help distract patients from the smell of the office. If you still struggle with the distinct odor of a dental office because of past experiences, you may want to bring along a flower or some other object that appeals to your sense of smell. This other scent will help you adjust to the office scent faster and you will also begin to correlate this smell to a positive experience. Children may benefit from this "odor replacement" as well.

"The Shot"

So, you've adjusted to the smell of the dentist's office, and now you've settled into the dental chair and are waiting to have a cavity filled. What happens next is critical because if certain steps in dental treatment are mishandled, the world may add another dental phobic to its total. I know for a fact that many adults have never gone back to a dentist because of their bad experiences.

One of the common bad experiences is "the shot." I have a childhood memory of getting an injection of Novocain from my dentist. Back then, one "patient management" technique involved saying, "This won't hurt a bit," as the dentist had the assistant use one hand to hold you down and the other to pass the needle in front of your eyes. Early on, I learned that when viewed up close in a dental office many things tend to look much larger than they actually are. I know I estimated that needle as at least three feet long. The dentist proceeded to say, "Open wide," and I thought, *Where is he going to put that three-foot needle?* My dentist, with his soft, gentle hand, jammed the needle into the back of my mouth. Damn, that hurt! It could have instilled permanent fear.

Thank goodness dentistry has come a long way since then. Today, an injection with local anesthetic that numbs the area of the mouth the dentist will be working on is much less uncomfortable and traumatic. Here are some reasons you have no reason to fear:

- First, Novocain is not used any more because there are newer and better local anesthetics on the market.
- Second, the dentist uses topical anesthetic to numb the gum tissue prior to any injection. This topical anesthetic is gel-like and comes in many flavors (mint, cinnamon, and bubble gum to name a few) so it is not distasteful to the patient. The real pain of the dental injection is the needle piercing the gum. The topical anesthetic eliminates this pain because the gum tissue is numb.
- Third, once the needle penetrates the gum tissue, you feel only a sensation of pressure, because few pain receptor-type nerves exist in this bone region.
- Fourth, the local anesthetic is slowly placed into the site, which causes minimal discomfort.
- Fifth, dentists are well-trained in administrating anesthesia, so in most cases you should not even see the needle.
- Sixth, make sure that you have a light meal before a dental appointment in which local anes-

thesia will be given. This will help prevent your chances of feeling light-headed or passing out.

So, Will I Drool?

When you think of a numbed mouth, you probably can call up the classic picture of the drooling dental patient. In reality, however, local anesthetic injected on the upper arch of your mouth provides anesthesia only in the area to be treated. You will barely experience the sensation of profound numbness, yet you will be numb and the procedures are pain free. An injection on the lower arch makes the lip numb, but you won't drool or appear to have a fat lip.

The Drill

Most people dread the drill, usually because they have had a bad experience with it, which often dates back to their childhood. For most of us, the dental drill of our childhood was of slow speed and controlled with a foot pedal. Between this old-fashioned drill and poor anesthesia, removing a cavity was not a comfortable treatment for patients. This treatment approach would scare *me* away from dentistry.

I am happy to report that the dental drill has come along way. The efficiency of the high-speed drill allows for quicker and more efficient dental treatment. However, there is that issue of the sound that won't go away-at least not yet. If you're nervous, the high-pitched sound of the drill can make for an uncomfortable experience. The high-speed drill works by air driving the rotation of the turbine, hence that noise. But remember that the noise has no correlation to pain.

To better cope with the noise, I recommend that you bring your MP3 (digital music, for those of you not hip to this term) or CD player with a headset. This may calm you down because your music will reduce the sound of the drill. If headphones don't work for you, then the good news is that we've seen recent advances in the technology of the dental drill. Manufacturers now make an electric high-speed drill, in which the turbine that spins the bur (dental talk for drill bit) is electric and not air. This method drastically reduces the noise and increases the performance of the drill.

Those who still have trouble facing any kind of drill will be happy to learn that recent advances in lasers and air-abrasion (which uses fine sand-like particles) instruments are being used for certain dental procedures and this eliminates the high-speed drill altogether.

Chapter Six

• • •

HOW SAFE *IS* THIS PLACE?

Another reason many people avoid the dentist is safety. Most people are concerned about going to the hospital or about the need to have a blood transfusion. And these worries do not just revolve around the reasons a hospital visit might be necessary. Let's face it; many of us have heard about infections in hospitals and the possibility of contracting HIV (human immunodeficiency virus, the virus that causes AIDS, acquired immunodeficiency syndrome), through blood transfusions. These fears quite naturally translate to the dental office, and are added to already existing concerns about x-rays and water quality. I'll discuss each and you will see that for the most part, these concerns are unfounded.

I'll Have an Evian® Please

You may have read reports about the water quality in dental offices. These concerns are twofold:

1. The accumulation of biofilm (naturally occurring bacteria and fungi in water that form a layer on

the plumbing piping surface) in the dental water-lines, and

2. The cross-contamination of saliva between patients by the water syringe used by a dentist or hygienist to rinse a patient's mouth.

Water has naturally occurring bacteria and fungi that are not eliminated at the local water filtration plant. These microorganisms can grow and contaminate the water and can accumulate in home plumbing, too. In dentistry, the concern revolves around the potential for microbes to grow in the waterline and then be sprayed into a patient's mouth. To date, no research exists that links infection with these bacteria and fungi. In addition, the American Dental Association has made recommendations to its members to flush the waterlines with an anti-microbial agent between patients.

Cross-contamination of saliva between patients is virtually impossible. You can take comfort in knowing that a dentist uses disposable syringe tips and anti-retraction devices that prevent a person's saliva from being sucked back up into the syringe from the reverse pressure that is created.

If you have these concerns about water quality in your dentist's office, simply ask the dental assistant or dentist about it. Most dental offices are more than happy to explain their water quality program and procedure.

Concerns About X-rays

X-rays are still the only way to detect dental disease below the gum line or inside a tooth. I will discuss the type of x-rays usually performed. However, most adults are concerned about repeated exposure to radiation. Radiation is pure energy; therefore it is not something that can be detected by any of the human senses. The fact is, we are all exposed to radiation on a daily basis. This everyday radiation can come from a number of sources, including one as simple as being outside. We also are exposed to radiation emitted by our home appliances, such as a television.

Radiation is quantified in units of millisievert (mSV) that enable a comparison of radiation from our home or outside environment to that which we receive from dental or medical x-rays. Dental x-rays deliver a minimal amount of radiation as compared with medical x-rays and with radiation exposure in our everyday life. For example, a full-mouth series of dental x-rays (18 films) has an American Dental Association estimated radiation exposure of .150 mSV. A single view chest x-ray has an approximate radiation exposure of .80 mSV. On an average day outside a person is exposed to approximately .008 mSV of radiation from natural sources. Therefore each dental film taken (.008mSV) is the equivalent of one day's worth of natural radiation from the outside atmospheric environment.

Looking at the big picture, I encourage you to feel comfortable about getting dental x-rays. High-speed film and lead aprons that protect the body from unnecessary radiation are used routinely. In addition, an increasing number of dentists are beginning to bring digital x-ray technology into their office. This method cuts the radiation exposure in half, thereby delivering .004mSV per film.

Types of dental x-rays include:

Periapical x-ray: This shows a view of the entire tooth including the roots and the bone. This is good for looking for decay and infection, and to assess the amount of remaining bone around the tooth.

Bitewing x-ray: This view shows the crown portion of the tooth and is good for detecting decay on or between teeth.

Panoramic x-ray: An overall single x-ray view of the mouth, showing the entire upper and lower jaw, including the teeth, bone, and sinuses. It is not as detailed as a bitewing or periapical x-ray and is often used in orthodontics or oral surgery.

Lateral Cephalometric x-ray: This is used primarily by orthodontists and oral surgeons to view the teeth in relation to the skeletal structures of the face.

A full series of dental x-rays (combination of periapical and bitewing x-rays) should be taken approximately every 18 months. It is not uncommon for a dentist to take a periapical or bitewing x-ray during a six-month recall appointment to check a specific area of concern.

Infection Control and the Dental Office

If there is one thing that modern dentistry has eliminated, it is the poor history of proper infection control in the dental office. Not too many years ago, dentists stuck their bare hands in your mouth. The dentist and auxiliary staff would never wear a mask
unless they were sick. The operatory was wiped down
with alcohol, while very few instruments were ever
heat sterilized in an *autoclave* (sterilization oven).

This has changed dramatically. Today's dental
offices use standard infection control as defined by
and for the medical community. For many reasons,
the standards are far higher than ever before.
Dentists must follow strict guidelines mandated
from governmental agencies like the Occupational
Safety and Health Administration (OSHA), the
Centers for Disease Control and Prevention (CDC),
and the Environmental Protection Agency (EPA).
There can also be separate state mandates.

Within a dental office setting, patients, dentists,
and dental staff could potentially be exposed to a
variety of microorganisms via oral, blood, or respira-
tory pathways. The major bacteria and viruses are
hepatitis B and C, herpes simplex, human immunodeficiency virus (HIV), tuberculosis bacteria, staphy-
lococci or streptococci bacteria, to name a few.

Because infectious diseases such as hepatitis B
and C and HIV cannot be easily identified in a
patient's medical history, the CDC recommends that

dental offices treat all patients *as if they have these diseases.* This means that the high level of infection control within a dental office must be constant and not change, even when dentists and staff are as good as certain that a particular patient does not have any infectious disease. In other words, dentists, just like all medical personnel today, avoid all contact with human blood and use protective gloves, even when they are confident the patient is not infected with HIV or hepatitis B or C or any other infection. They follow this protocol regardless of extenuating circumstances.

The following lists key elements of standard dental office protocol. I trust it will reassure you that you, along with dentists and staff, are protected from any possible infectious disease.

- The Centers for Disease Control and Prevention recommends that dental healthcare workers be immunized for hepatitis B virus.
- Dental healthcare workers should wear protective clothing and barriers such as gloves, masks and protective eyewear.
- Disposable covers are placed on items in the dental operatory that are at risk for being contaminated with blood or saliva, or by equipment, such as a laptop computer, that can not be disinfected due to the possibility of mechanical damage.
- The Occupational Safety and Health Administration (OSHA) requires that disposable needles, scalpels, or any other sharp instruments

be placed into a "sharps" container that is resistant to puncture or hand placement. Solid waste that is contaminated should be sealed in a plastic bag specially made for biohazardous waste. Local, state, or federal governments regulate the protocol for disposal of these solid waste bags. All other non-disposable instruments need to be heat sterilized.

- The Environmental Protection Agency (EPA) requires manufacturers to label a chemical germicide that is used in a dental office as "hospital disinfectant" and labeled as "tuberculocidal." Mycobacterium tuberculosis bacteria are among the most resistant groups of microorganisms. This germicide solution is used to wipe the operatory down after each patient. This includes the countertops, dental chair, and so forth.
- Dentist and staff must wash their hands frequently with antibacterial soap.

A dental patient can feel "safe" in the majority of dental offices because these numerous mandated precautions protect against infectious disease and consensus exists among government agencies and the ADA about their value. Government standards of infection control make it almost impossible for a patient or dental health-care worker to become infected with bacteria or viruses. Should you notice that these protocols are not followed, then consider it a signal that the particular practice is not in the mainstream of "safe" dentistry. The next time you're "offended" by the "sterile" smell of a dental office, remember that the strict infection control is "defending" you against infectious diseases.

Chapter Seven

• • •

TAKING THE HELL OUT OF A ROOT CANAL

You may recall that I decided to specialize in endodontics and proudly told my mother I'd been given one of the most sought after positions in a residency program. Rather than patting me on the back and telling me I was the greatest ever, she immediately thought "root canal" and therefore, "pain." I should have expected that response. More than any other dental procedure, the root canal is used to describe any experience that is almost "the worst of the worst," the very worst, of course, being reserved for this particular treatment. We know something is bad when people say they'd rather have a root canal than do it. From childbirth to testifying before Congress to an IRS audit, a root canal is preferable. This joke is still alive because the truth about root canal treatments has not broken through the myths.

Times have changed drastically. To paraphrase the Hair Club for Men slogan ("I'm not just the president, but I am a member too!") I am not just an endodontist, but also someone who has had endodontic treatment. I had my first root canal treatment when I was 13 years old, and I still remember the pain. My last root canal treatment was a little over a year ago and not only was it quick, I had no discomfort during or after the procedure.

So, root canal treatment has come a long way, and if you had a bad experience with it, that probably stemmed from poor pain control in conjunction with inefficient instruments used to perform the actual treatment. Today, the field of endodontics (root canals) has better methods of pain control, high tech instrumentation, and visualization that allows a dentist to use a camera the size of a pin to look down into the tooth. For the most part, having root canal treatment today is no different than having a cavity filled.

Regardless of recent advances, most people still want to know the answers to four fundamental questions:

1. *Why would I need a root canal?*

   To remove inflamed or infected nerve tissue from within a tooth and/or to enable a dentist to build up a broken tooth by placing a post into the root. This allows the dentist to rebuild a tooth's crown portion and fit a new crown over it.

2. *How many office visits does a root canal involve?*

   At one time, it took 3-4 office visits, but with new advances in endodontics, root canal treatment usually involves 1-2 appointments.

3. *Why is it called a "root canal?"*

   I am sure if you surveyed a group of people and

asked them to define a root canal, they may say it is the nerve of the tooth or it is somewhere in a tooth. Some may even say that they do not know the answer, but they've heard it's painful so they don't care to know. A "root canal" is just what it states. Each tooth has a root or roots that extend from the crown portion. The root or roots have a space within them that is called a canal. The canal houses the nerve and blood supply for the tooth. (See Figure 3A)

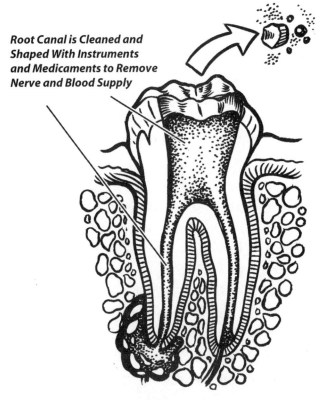

Root Canal is Cleaned and Shaped With Instruments and Medicaments to Remove Nerve and Blood Supply

Root Canal Treatment - Figure 3A.

4. *Why have root canal treatment when the tooth could be extracted?*

   Although sometimes the best treatment is to extract a tooth and replace it with a bridge or implant, a root canal is a good treatment option for the following reasons:

   • Fibers that hold the tooth to the bone are called periodontal ligaments. Nerves around these ligaments that are called *proprioceptors*. These are sensory nerves that give information concerning movements and position of the teeth and mouth to the brain. An implant will not have any of these types of sensory nerves.

   • Bridges used to replace missing teeth often involve the reduction of the two teeth that are immediately adjacent to the edentulous space.

   The exception would be a "Maryland Bridge," which is commonly used for the replacement of anterior teeth. The adjacent teeth have a preparation on the back side of the tooth and are not reduced.

   • Although implants can be a good alternative treatment for replacing a missing tooth, there is sometimes a misconception among patients that implants can be completed in one or two visits to the dentist. In fact, it can sometimes take up to a year to complete the implant and the placement of final crown over the implant to be completed. Remember that the bone must incorporate into the implant for it to be stable.

- On average, a root canal will cost less than a bridge or implant.

It is always best to try and keep the original part that you were given at the factory! Just like in medicine, a replacement knee or hip or limb is never the same as the original.

What the Actual Treatment Involves

The procedure "officially" begins when the dentist numbs the patient's tooth, at which point he or she will place what is called a *rubber dam* over the tooth needing root canal treatment. This isolates the tooth and prevents saliva from getting into the actual root canal space, and also keeps the medication used during the procedure from getting into the patient's mouth.

Assuming you're the patient anticipating a root canal, you will be able to breathe comfortably when the rubber dam is on. The dentist will then make a small opening in the back of your tooth if it is a front tooth or on the top of the tooth if it is a back tooth. The actual root canal treatment involves removing the nerve and blood supply from within the tooth. This is accomplished with very small instruments called files. In conjunction with the files, the dentist will use a solution of sodium hypochlorite (very diluted) to help remove the nerve tissue. After the canal has been cleaned and prepared, the dentist fills the

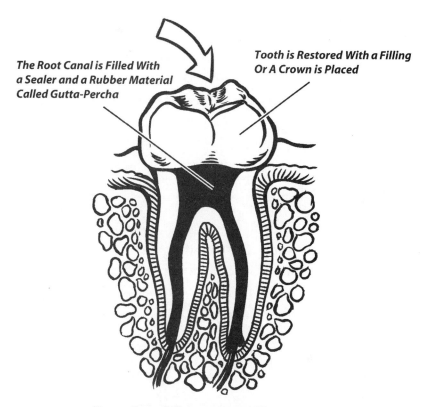

The Root Canal is Filled With a Sealer and a Rubber Material Called Gutta-Percha

Tooth is Restored With a Filling Or A Crown is Placed

Root Canal Treatment - Figure 3B.

empty space created from the files with an inert rubber material called *gutta-percha* and *sealer* (similar to dental cement). And that's it! (See Figure 3B)

The remainder of the procedure involves restoring the tooth, which is accomplished either by placing a permanent filling in the access (the small hole made by the dentist to get into the root canal) or by placing a crown on the tooth.

The above explanation covers conventional root canal treatment, which means that the tooth is opened through its crown portion to access the tooth's root canal space within its root structure. There are cases when a conventional root canal has been completed and a crown or filling is intact (meaning no points of leakage). However, in these cases an infection persists or reoccurs around the tooth after root canal treatment. The cause of the infection is usually a preexisting infection that never healed, even after the root canal treatment was completed. Sometimes, although the root canal treatment is completed, the body cannot fight the infection that is around the tooth, and healing doesn't take place. In these cases, "surgical" root canal treatment is performed. This involves the *reflection* (cutting and bringing the gum tissue off the jawbone) of the gum tissue over the tooth in question and removing the infection around the root end of the tooth. This can involve the *resection* (the removal of the bottom 2-3mm of the root) of a small portion of the root and the placement of a filling material (root end fill) into the end of the tooth's root to help seal the tooth from further infection. (See Figure 4A, 4B, 4C)

To allow proper healing, the gum tissue is placed back into position with stitches. The advantage of this procedure is that it is usually performed under local anesthesia and is completed in one patient visit, without the need to remove the crown or filling and

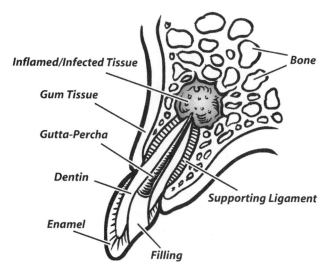

Root Canal Surgery Procedure - Figure 4A.

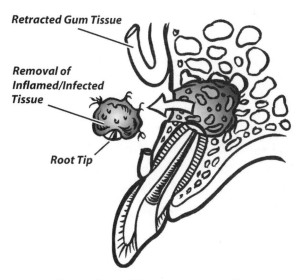

Root Canal Surgery Procedure - Figure 4B.

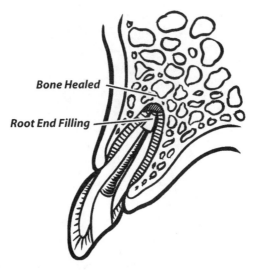

Bone Healed

Root End Filling

Root Canal Surgery Procedure - Figure 4C.

root canal filling (gutta-percha and sealer) that was previously placed.

Surgical root canal treatment is performed only in cases where a crown or filling is intact. In cases when there is infection after root canal treatment has been completed in the past, but the crown or filling is not intact, a dentist may recommend "retreatment" of the root canal. This means redoing the root canal with conventional treatment and removing the old root canal filling material and replacing it with new material to better seal the tooth from infection. A new crown or filling is then placed on a tooth after root canal retreatment is completed.

Eliminating the Myths of Root Canal Treatment

Besides all the jokes about root canals, abundant misinformation about them exists, too. This misinformation comes primarily from holistic physicians and dentists. I have nothing against this type of healthcare thought, but as a professor of endodontics (root canal treatment) I do find it troublesome when legitimate scientific information is twisted and then communicated to the general public in such a way as to cause unnecessary concern of having root canal treatment.

Over the last few years, information disseminated on the Internet and in books often uses outdated and flawed scientific research to scare patients about the dangers of having a root canal treated tooth. The primary point of contention is that there is a belief among a group of holistic healthcare providers that a *necrotic* (a situation in which nerve and vascular tissue dies off) tooth or a tooth that has had previous endodontic treatment can cause disease in other parts of the body. The term for this is *focal infection theory* and dates back to the late 1800s. At that time, it was thought that these "dead" teeth contain bacteria that could get out around the tooth and travel via the blood stream to other parts of the body, thereby setting up the conditions in which other medical conditions can develop. At the time the solution was to remove any tooth that needed root canal treatment so the patient could avoid becoming severely ill or even die! At the turn of the century, dentists and physicians believed that these "infected teeth" were the cause of many medical ailments and disease.

Since the late 1930s, good scientific research has proven the focal infection theory to be false. First, scientists demonstrated that the removal of these "diseased" teeth did not cure a patient's particular medical disease or ailment. Secondly, they found that the infection in the tooth was actually walled off by the body to prevent any spread of infection. Lastly, researchers have not found any cause-effect relationship of root canal infections to systemic disease. Unfortunately, there are still a few dentists and physicians in this century that continue to support the focal infection theory and try to convince their patients on the "evil" of root canal treatment.

Today, researchers continue to report in scientific journals that the focal infection theory has no merit. Looking back at the early research supporting focal infection, present day researchers have found that turn-of-the-century scientific protocol governing research in this area was extremely flawed. The reality is that root canal treatment is a safe and an effective way to remove inflamed or infected nerve and vascular tissue from a tooth. Patients today have the great benefit of keeping these treated teeth in their mouths for many years without concern over systemic disease.

As a matter of science, a tooth that is inflamed (meaning that the person shows sensitivity to temperature on a particular tooth) shows no evidence of bacterial infection. The blood supply and lymphatic fluid within the tooth act as antibacterial agents, thus preventing bacteria from entering the tooth. A tooth that is labeled necrotic (meaning that the nerve and vascular tissue has died) can harbor bacteria within the actual root canals. The clinical signs and symptoms of a necrotic tooth can be soreness when biting down on the tooth, swelling, or signs on x-rays of an infection around the roots demonstrated by bone loss. However, modern-day root canal treatment can remove the infection with mechanical and medicament intervention from within the tooth and allow the body to properly heal the bone area around the tooth.

It is also important to understand that root canal morphology is very complex. Therefore, the holistic dentist will argue that this makes it impossible for a dentist doing root canal treatment to remove all the inflamed or infected tissue, thus creating a risk of causing harm to the rest of the body. Although root canal systems are complex, modern dentistry is able to use medication during a root canal procedure that can reach these small areas within a tooth that the mechanical aspect of treatment can't. The sealer portion of the filling material (remember gutta-percha and sealer are used to fill the root canal space) also has the ability to flow in to the small areas within a tooth; because of its chemical composition the filling material can eliminate bacteria and toxins.

Adventures of a Endodontic Resident

During the first two months of my residency in endodontics I often asked myself what the hell I did. I was living like a college student again only putting in longer hours. As I ate cereal for dinner, I longed for the days when I had my general dentistry practice. At times I began to think that my mother might have been right—I should have left well enough alone. But after the first three months or so, time began to go by faster, and I began finding the program exciting and challenging.

At the beginning of my second year of residency I was completing my research in laser endodontics and was doing a dog study at the University of Wisconsin, School of Veterinary Medicine. My master's degree thesis advisor was Dr. Paul Howard, Professor and Chairman of the Department of Surgery. Paul called me one day and said he and some other veterinarians from the surgery department were going to do a root canal on a polar bear at the local zoo in Madison, Wisconsin. He also went on to say that he volunteered me to assist because he thought the laser might be helpful during the procedure.

I arrived at the zoo on a muggy August morning. The large polar bear had been put to sleep by the vet anesthesiologist and was laid out on a few bails of hay on the rock portion of the bear's outdoor habitat. I hadn't known that when you work on the oral cavity of an animal you should be on the animal's backside. As the rookie vet dentist, I started to work on the oral cavity from the wrong side. The problem with this is if animals, like the polar bear, get a little light under anesthesia they can move their paws, which in the case of the bear, includes very large claws. Well, needless to say, the bear got light under anesthesia and swiped its paw past me, just missing my exposed thigh. I'm a quick study, so I immediately changed my position.

Overall, the procedure went well, but I quickly realized that bear dentistry is not an easy task. Between the bad ergonomics, the August heat, the bear's fur, and the constant buzz of flies around my head, I sweated my butt off. After completing the work, the surgical team carted the sleeping bear back to its indoor cage. Then the anesthesiologist asked me to help give the reversing agent. My job was to pull the IV (intravenous) line after the injection was given in the animal's rear. The vet told me that when he gave the word, I should run for the cage door, but under no circumstances should I look back.

Of course, at that moment I knew human nature was going to take over and I was certainly going to look back. As the vet gave the command to run like hell for the door, I pulled the IV drip and ran for it, but just as I gave in and looked back, I saw the bear quickly jump to its feet and move around as in a drunken stupor. The bear's actions sent a jolt of fear through my body that froze my muscles, making me feel as if I was running in slow motion. As I got through the door some 10 yards away from the bear, the vet slammed the cage door and then secured the large padlock. As my breathing and blood pressure returned to normal, I realized that my zoo dentistry days were over. To this day, I can't take my kids to the zoo without having my heart beat a little faster when we walk by the polar bear exhibit.

Chapter Eight

• • •

SWEET DREAMS AT THE DENTIST, OR WAKE ME WHEN IT'S OVER

Many people are afraid to be awake during dental procedures. They may have consulted with their long-standing family dentist about various forms of anesthesia, but perhaps were told they would be just fine with local anesthesia. However, in reality, this may not be true. The reason many older dentists do not offer various forms of anesthesia is that they have never been trained in methods other than local anesthetics.

From an overall time and financial perspective, it is advantageous if patients feel comfortable with a local anesthetic, but it is perfectly all right to require nitrous oxide, oral sedation, intravenous (IV) sedation, or general anesthesia. Ironically, general anesthesia was actually invented in 1846 by a Boston dentist named Dr. William T.G. Morton, yet dentistry has never embraced it for their patients the way medicine has.

Before you make any decision about anesthesia beyond local anesthesia, it's important that you understand the range of options and their relative advantages and disadvantages.

Nitrous Oxide: This involves inhaling a combination of nitrous oxide and oxygen. This gas allows you to feel euphoric, yet fully awake and conscious.

Advantages:

- The dentist can safely administer it.
- You maintain all your protective reflexes such as gagging and coughing.
- Nitrous oxide and oxygen is administered through a mask that is placed over your nose. It does not require IV (intravenous lines) like other sedation methods or general anesthesia.
- This method has minimal risk.
- You will need minimum postoperative recovering time, meaning that you'll have no side effects and you can leave the dental office without any one having to accompany you home.

Disadvantages:

- Local anesthesia is needed in combination with nitrous oxide.
- There is usually an additional anesthesia fee.

Oral Sedation: This involves taking prescribed sedating medication such as Valium® or Halcion® before going to the dentist. This allows you to feel relaxed and free of stress.

Advantages:

- Easy to administer (swallowing only 1-2 pills, depending on which medication is prescribed).

Normal dosage range of Valium is 5-10 mg and of Halcion is 0.125-0.25 mg.

- You usually take it 60 minutes prior to a dental appointment.
- You will not lose consciousness and you will maintain all physiological functions such as normal breathing, gag, and coughing reflexes.
- This sedation involves minimal risk.
- Its cost is insignificant.

Disadvantages:

- You will need someone with you because you cannot drive to and from the dental office while under the influence of the medication.
- Depending on the individual, it can take a few hours after dental treatment to eliminate the drug from the body.
- You will still need local anesthesia.

Conscious IV Sedation: This involves the use of medication delivered through intravenous injection. It minimally depresses your level of consciousness, which allows you to be relaxed and in a state of light or "twilight' sleep.

Advantages:

- You are able to breathe on your own and can respond to voice commands. The body's defense mechanisms such as gagging and cough reflexes are not affected from this type of sedation.
- You enter a deeper sleep state than that achieved

with the use of nitrous oxide or oral sedation medication.

- The medication that is administered allows that patient when they awaken not to have any specific recollection of dental treatment.

  Disadvantages:

- Preoperative prep is the same as if you were having general anesthesia, meaning no food or drink after midnight the previous evening.
- Your recovery time can be 30-60 minutes after the procedure and you will need to stay at the dentist's office during that time. You may feel groggy and you'll need the time to allow the medication to clear your body.
- Because of the after-effects of the medication, you will need someone to accompany you home.
- This method may add considerable cost to your dental treatment.
- This method carries a moderate risk because of possible complications from drugs given for sedation.

General Anesthesia: You lose consciousness, just as you would if you had surgery anywhere else on the body under general anesthesia.

  Advantages:

- You are in a deep sleep state during dental treatment.

  Disadvantages:

- You lose control of your reflexes and the ability to

breathe on your own. A breathing tube is placed through the nose and then down the throat to assist your breathing.

- Must be administered in a hospital or surgicenter.
- You need a longer recovery period, compared to IV sedation.
- This method carries greater risk than IV sedation anesthesia because of the type of drugs given.
- Cost for general anesthesia alone can be more expensive than the actual dental procedure.

Who Does What?

Most of today's dentists are trained to provide local anesthesia, nitrous oxide, and oral sedation to their patients. These three techniques effectively control pain while being relatively safe, meaning that there is only a low risk of complication.

If you believe you may require anesthesia methods beyond these three simple methods, then ask your dentist the following questions about general anesthesia or IV sedation.

1. *Who will administer and monitor the general anesthesia?*

I recommend a board-certified anesthesiologist if general anesthesia is given. An anesthesiologist is a medical doctor who has completed a minimum of four years of residency training in anesthesia. Since this procedure is performed in a hospital or state certified surgicenter, an anesthesiologist will be on staff. Do not have general anesthesia performed in a dental office or clinic. A hospital or surgicenter is better equipped to provide and monitor patients under general anesthesia.

2. *Who will administer and monitor the IV sedation?* If you are receiving IV sedation, it is commonly performed in a dental office or clinic setting. Ask who on staff has been trained to administer the sedation. This training involves a minimum of two years of formal training beyond dental school and certification in IV anesthesia. This does not mean a weekend course on sedation given at a luxury golf and spa resort!

As in other professions, dentistry has many opportunities for a dentist to stay current with changes in the field by taking CE (continuing education) classes, usually held on weekends. Some states require dentists to take a certain amount of CE courses to maintain their state license. These courses are good for learning new types of tooth filling materials or how to become better as a cosmetic dentist, for example. When it comes to advanced procedures and techniques like giving anesthesia, one must receive a formal education as mentioned above. It is impossible for a dentist to become proficient in anesthesia after taking a weekend course. After a dentist receives formal training in anesthesia, then a weekend CE course only enables them to stay abreast with the changes in the field.

Usually an oral surgeon, nurse anesthetist (a registered nurse with a minimum of two years of anesthesia training after completion of a nursing degree), or a dental anesthesiologist (a dentist who has completed a medical anesthesia residency after dental school) should provide IV-sedation in your dentist's office. He or she will also be responsible for bringing all the necessary drugs and monitoring equipment so that the anesthesia procedure can be safely carried out in the dental office or clinic.

Although some dentists have received formal training in IV sedation anesthesia, it is not recommended that the dentist be both the surgeon and the anesthesiologist. It is still important that a nurse anesthetist monitor the patient.

If a dentist tells you that there is no problem providing IV sedation and performing the procedure, too, be on alert. This is not acceptable! In addition, be suspicious about the actual anesthesia training the dentist received. In this day and age, any person with formal IV sedation training understands that another individual must monitor a patient while undergoing dental treatment.

3. *What is the state licensing requirement for pro-*

viding anesthesia in a dental office?
State requirements vary, but generally include training in a proper setting and meeting state certification guidelines. In addition, the facility must provide required monitoring equipment, along with emergency drugs.

4. *Is there a recovery area within the office or clinic?*
Although it is acceptable to use the dental chair as a recovery area, a separate area allows you to recover from the anesthesia without feeling rushed. Sometimes a busy office or clinic without a designated recovery area may send the patient home earlier than is optimal after advanced anesthesia is administered.

5. *Does Insurance cover any of the anesthesia procedure?*
Most medical insurance policies cover certain dental procedures with the use of IV sedation or general anesthesia.

If after talking to your dentist you still have reservations or questions about advanced forms of anesthesia, seek a second opinion. If you feel pressured or "smooth talked" by a dentist, it is probably someone who isn't qualified to provide advanced anesthesia in the first place. Remember that your personal well-being is at risk, and you can't take the anesthesia issue lightly. Although the chance of problems developing during anesthesia is small, you want the person administering the anesthesia to be qualified to treat you with the necessary emergency drugs.

So...

You have other options besides local anesthesia, and I realize that it may seem difficult to make the right decision. However, after 17 years as a dentist, I can conclude that about 95 percent of patients undergoing routine dental treatment (fillings, root canals, gum treatment, and simple extractions) will be comfortable with local anesthetic alone or local anesthetic in combination with nitrous oxide or oral sedation. That means that only about 5 percent of patients need IV sedation or general anesthesia. Generally, IV sedation is administered during a more invasive dental procedure or one that takes considerable time, such as implants, extraction of wisdom teeth, extensive gum surgery, or extensive crown and bridge work.

General anesthesia is usually given to patients who have physical or mental handicaps. In addition, general anesthesia is used with patients undergoing *orthognathic* surgery (this involves the movement of the upper and/or the lower jaw). Orthognathic surgery is done for cosmetic or functional reasons, meaning better occlusion, that is, the way the teeth come together in the mouth.

Overall, the use of different levels of anesthesia in dentistry should parallel the levels of anesthesia used for certain medical procedures. For example, if you see a dermatologist to have a skin lesion treated then a local anesthetic will adequately control the pain. But if you needed an appendectomy, you would not agree to local anesthesia! Obviously, you'd receive general anesthesia.

Always remember that the more advanced the anesthesia, the greater your risk, and it's your responsibility to evaluate the risk-benefit ratio. The greater benefit of general anesthesia outweighs the risk when an appendectomy is necessary, but the opposite is true when removing your skin lesion because local anesthesia is all that's needed to perform this relatively painless procedure.

Now that you have this information, if you still believe you'll need general anesthesia to have your teeth cleaned, then I recommend seeking therapy to help you constructively deal with your fear of and anxiety about dental treatment. That would be a far more productive way to spend your money than accepting the risk of advanced anesthesia in order to have cleaner teeth!

Chapter Nine

. . .

HONK IF YOU LOVE YOUR DENTAL HYGIENIST, OR NOW THAT WE HAVE YOU HERE

As those who have regular dental care know, one of the first procedures performed on new patients is a thorough cleaning of their teeth and gums. Although some dentists do this job themselves, most have dental hygienists as part of the dental office team. The dental hygienist has received a minimum of two years of training after high school. Today, most hygienists are college graduates with a Bachelor of Science degree in dental hygiene.

Hygienists remove plaque and calculus from the teeth and gum tissue. There is usually no anesthetic involved, although patients with sensitivity due to poor hygiene may require some topical anesthesia, which is the same flavored gel applied to the gum tissue before administering a numbing shot of local anesthesia. Some hygienists use an ultrasonic instrument that can remove the plaque and calculus quickly and efficiently, usually without much discomfort to the patient. Then your teeth are also flossed and polished with special professional-strength toothpaste. This type of toothpaste has more cleaning abrasives than toothpaste that you purchase in a store. These abrasives help to clean the stains from your teeth, making them appear whiter.

The dental hygienist may take some x-rays if the dentist has not already taken them at the consult appointment. The hygienist will then educate you on how to properly brush and floss at home. After the hygienist is finished, the dentist will come in the treatment room to check your mouth and discuss any further treatment that may be necessary.

If You're Anxious...

When you're treated by the dental hygienist first, you know exactly what is going to happen at this dental appointment. You understand that the only treatment you're going to have is a cleaning of your teeth and gums and possibly some x-rays. Hygienists are not licensed to perform any further dental procedures. A patient can bring a music player with headphones to the hygiene appointment to help make it a good experience.

I personally picked a dentist who has a TV hanging on the wall in the hygiene room. I schedule appointments for my tooth and gum cleaning at a time when I can watch ESPN *Sport Center* during the procedure.

This makes my own trip to the dentist a positive one.

The great thing about a cleaning appointment is that you leave with a fresh feeling and a good taste in your mouth, which helps imprint the idea that going to the dentist can be a positive experience. The fresh feeling can be a motivating factor for the dental phobic patient to keep up good oral hygiene at home. The typical patient has two professional hygiene appointments a year. This is optimal for maintaining good oral health. (Once again this is not a conspiracy by the dental profession to make money, but is based on research about maintaining healthy gums and teeth.)

Does Gum Disease Come From Chewing Gum?

Strange as it seems, some people believe this. However, gum disease comes from *plaque* and *calculus*. Plaque is a soft material that is made up of bacteria and food debris. When the plaque is not removed and minerals from saliva interact with it, the plaque hardens and becomes calculus. Plaque and calculus can cause decay in teeth and irritate gum tissue, thereby causing gum disease.

The technical term for gum disease is *periodontal* disease: *perio* means gums and *dontal* refers to teeth. This disease affects the gum tissue and is characterized by irritation and redness. When gum disease advances unchecked, it affects the bone and ligaments that hold a tooth in its socket. (See Figure 5)

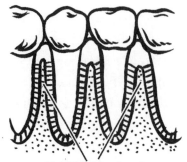

Healthy Bone Level

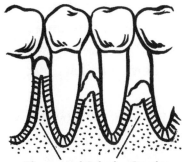

**Plaque and Calculus Causing
Reduction of Bone Around Teeth**

**Plaque and Calculus Causing
Reduction of Bone
Around Teeth - Figure 5.**

Gingivitis is the early stage of periodontal disease, and its signs include redness, slight swelling, and bleeding after brushing and flossing. When gingivitis is left untreated it causes the gum to begin receding from the tooth, at which point it enters the stage called *periodontitis*. When the bone and ligaments become inflamed and infected, the gum disease is referred to as advanced periodontitis.

Bleeding and swelling of the gum tissue, pain, pus from the gums, halitosis (see definition below), and loose teeth mark this advanced stage of gum disease.

Once again, the further the disease is allowed to progress, the poorer the chances of keeping a tooth affected by periodontal disease. Early intervention by a general dentist or a periodontist (a dentist who specializes in treating diseased gums) will greatly enhance the patient's chances of keeping their teeth.

The main reason gum disease has become so prevalent in the US population is related to the fact that people are living longer with their natural teeth. Increased life expectancy, combined with better oral health care, has meant fewer tooth extractions than in previous generations. Although daily personal oral hygiene is performed by most Americans, many people still avoid visits to the dentist. This avoidance lends it self to allowing oral disease like gum disease to go unchecked. With proper oral health care, many men and women can maintain healthy teeth and gums over a lifetime. This is an important reason why people who avoid the dentist due to dental anxiety and fear should seek help in order to overcome these hurdles.

Hal-it-o-sis

Halitosis is the technical term for bad breath, and those who fear oral health care usually fall victim to it because their oral hygiene habits are not adequate to fight the cause of bad breath. Most people fear bad breath and put it right up there with body odor as a "social offense." The reality is that bad breath can penetrate well out of a person's two to three foot personal zone. If you live in a cold climate, try exhaling air when it's cold and you might be surprised how far your breath travels! Because this is an intensely personal issue, most people, even family and close friends, often are too uncomfortable to tell the person about the bad breath. This is why services exist that actually send anonymous letters to individuals to discreetly inform them of their halitosis.

Men and women who avoid professional dental care, including regular teeth and gum cleaning, usually say they brush their teeth every night and floss at least occasionally. Unfortunately, this is not enough to fight bad breath. Brushing teeth and gums that are diseased from lack of professional oral care is like putting a fresh coat of paint on a rusty old car before removing the rust. It may seem like the car is new, but it's only a matter of time before the rust eats through the paint and the car falls apart.

Bad breath originates from the breakdown of food by bacteria in the mouth. Remember that over 300 different species of bacteria exist in our oral cavity, many of which are called normal flora, meaning that they naturally co-exist with the other cells in our body without causing problems. Some of these bacteria require oxygen to live and are referred to as aerobic bacteria (not the kind seen in working out in the gym!); bacteria that survive in a no- or low-oxygen environment are called anaerobic.

Oral bacteria live on the teeth, the gum tissue, and the tongue. Aerobic bacteria live on the surface where the oxygen is plentiful while the anaerobic bacteria live in between teeth and gums and in the deep crevices of the tongue where there is less oxygen available. Bacteria survive by using their biochemical make-up to break down food particles for energy. They especially love carbohydrates and other sugars. Waste by-products of the food particles are released back into the mouth; these are the agents that cause bad breath.

Sweet and sensuous movie and television scenes aside, most of us often wake up in the morning with bad breath. While you're catching 40 winks, bacteria are up all night partying in your mouth. When you awake, your mouth is like the morning after a freshman dorm party. It feels like beer bottles and cigarette butts are strewn all over the place.

When oral hygiene is poor, food not properly removed from the mouth can literally decay and give off an odor. This is like forgetting there's a sanitation strike in your town and leaving your trash on the curb for pick-up. Days pass, and the smell isn't pretty! Another way we get halitosis is by eating certain foods, like garlic or onions. These foods are absorbed into the bloodstream and then when the blood passes through the lungs, the odor the foods produce is exhaled. A common misconception among those who have plaque and calculus build-up (another cause of bad breath) is that brushing, flossing and mouth-wash will eliminate these oral odors. In truth, these actions may temporarily mask the smell, but the odor will continue until the mouth is cleaned profes-sionally by a hygienist or a dentist. In between these appointments, halitosis will be eliminated with good daily oral hygiene habits.

Halitosis can be a warning sign for gum disease or other medical disorders such as postnasal drip from sinusitis, gastrointestinal reflux, and liver or kidney disease. Dentists should refer patients for further medical care if their oral health is good but they continue to have bad breath. However, other medical disorders aside, if you commit to seeing an oral hygienist every six months, along with continu-ing regular brushing and flossing in between dentist visits, you likely will be free of bad breath.

Chapter Ten

• • •

THAT TOOTH HAS TO GO

In modern dentistry, we always try to save a patient's natural teeth—the ones installed at the factory. But even with all the technology available, not all teeth can be saved. Simple extractions are usually done by the general dentist and more complicated extractions (teeth impacted in the bone or severely broken down from decay) are usually performed by an oral surgeon.

If you are afraid of this procedure, ask your dentist to explain the type and amount of anesthesia you will receive in order to avoid experiencing any pain. If you are under local anesthetic you should feel only a pressure sensation, and if you are asleep from IV sedation, then of course you won't feel anything. (You are welcome to keep the extracted tooth and you can put it under your pillow and hope the tooth fairy arrives. Although my kids still believe in the tooth fairy, I must admit that I don't like the idea of any stranger entering my house at night while I am asleep!)

The area around the extraction will take about six weeks to heal. During this time a dentist can place a temporary tooth or teeth so that you don't walk around with missing teeth. After the extraction site is healed, you can choose permanent tooth restoration. Advances in dental materials allow the dentist to correctly match the shade and durability of these permanent replacement teeth to the patient's existing natural teeth.

What Happens Next?

After a tooth is extracted, it is important to replace it so that the mouth maintains normal function for eating, speaking, and overall facial muscle balance. In the "old days" of dentistry, you would usually have a removable full or partial denture to replace a tooth or teeth. This oral appliance was often difficult to adjust to, and if it replaced front teeth it was less than cosmetically optimal.

With the advances in today's dentistry, many new tooth replacements are permanently fixed in the mouth. Even when your only alternative is to have a removable denture, newer treatment methods exist to better help secure the teeth so you can better adapt to the denture. (I'll discuss these treatments later in the book.)

More Dental School Adventures

A dental student never forgets the first time they actually pull a tooth. It is sort of a right of passage into the clinical phase of a student's training. My first tooth extraction experience was no different. I was on a rotation at Boston City Hospital, which was used as the basis for the 1980s NBC medical drama, *St. Elsewhere*. On my first morning in the oral surgery outpatient clinic, I wore a fresh pair of surgical scrubs and a brand new white lab coat. This professional outfit could not help but make me feel like I was a "real" dentist.

The patient that was scheduled for me that morning had been up all night with a bad toothache. He was tired, grumpy, and hurting—and these were some of his best qualities! I must have looked too rested and eager because the patient sensed that I was a rookie who was about to take out his badly decayed, non-restorable tooth. As my nervous, shaking hand gave the local anesthetic, the patient had to have noticed the beads of sweat accumulating on my forehead. The patient asked if I had ever taken out a tooth before, and I responded calmly, "Sure I have." I figured it made no sense to make us both nervous.

It was such a unique feeling to place my forceps on a tooth for the first time as I tried to remove this broken down tooth with confidence. I patiently worked the tooth out of the patient's mouth—it came out like a hot knife going through butter. As I held my first extracted tooth proudly in the forceps, I carefully placed it on the surgical tray. The sense of accomplishment made me flush with pride.

We were required to have the attending oral surgeon look at the patient and check off on a procedure. As my attending looked into my patient's mouth he quickly put down the mouth mirror and asked me to step out in to the hallway. I thought he was going to tell me what a great job I had done, but unfortunately, he explained that I had taken out the wrong tooth!

Luckily for me, the tooth I took out would have eventually needed to be extracted, because the decay was so extensive that the tooth was deemed non-restorable. The attending was a true professional. He took pity on me as a rookie dentist and didn't appear upset or mad, and he was a great teacher and worked with me to remove the correct tooth. He then explained the situation to the patient and did not charge him for the two extractions. The patient left happy, but I decided at that moment that I would have no plans in the immediate future to specialize in Oral Surgery!

Chapter Eleven

• • •

MILES OF SMILES

As you know, over the last couple of decades, Americans have become health conscious. At least, they collect mountains of information and believe they know what they *should* do! Along with health consciousness, concern about appearance has intensified, and procedures to reshape the body and get rid of wrinkles have become increasingly popular. But what good is a smooth face and a liposuctioned mid-section if you smile and show broken teeth, or even worse, gaps where teeth used to be? Without question, cosmetic treatment in dentistry has never received more attention than it does today. Cosmetic dentistry is part of our collective quest to appear youthful and confident, no matter what the date on our driver's license reveals.

Although statistically, a person's teeth are visible only 15 percent of the time, a missing tooth in an adult can be interpreted as a sign of age and is aesthetically displeasing. A missing front tooth can be so cosmetically displeasing that a person may experience job or professional discrimination because of it. Can you imagine a super model with bad teeth? No catalog or fashion magazine in the world would include her, or him, for that matter. Likewise, a person with similar dental problems is not likely to be made partner in a big law firm or even hired as its receptionist. Successful sales professionals almost always look the part, which does not allow for missing teeth. Considering a person's face is visible 100 percent of the time, missing, stained, or misaligned teeth can be more cosmetically noticeable than wrinkles or a facial mole.

Advances in cosmetic and aesthetic dentistry have been great and rapid. Space-age resins and porcelain and whitening agents have allowed dentists to dramatically change a person's smile. In addition, many of these cosmetic procedures can be performed with out any anesthetics.

Dentistry's Replacement Parts

One of the most difficult tasks in the medical sciences is replacing parts of the human body. Chemists may have estimated the "material" worth of our body parts at about $12, but we are biochemically complex creatures and making new "parts" is an ongoing challenge.

Most people now take for granted what is actually the incredible dental feat of replacing a vital body part: a tooth. The *prosthetic*-replacement-treatment that a dentist provides is unmatched in any other field of medicine. The dentist's ability to fabricate teeth that provide the same look and function as natural teeth has come a long way over the years. George Washington and his compatriots may have been forced to endure their wooden dentures (which were an advance, after all), but your dentist is working with you so you can keep your own teeth as long as possible.

Prosthetic dental treatment must take into consideration the volatile environment of the oral cavity, and both the dentist and the laboratory technician must work with great precision. Consider that a crown, bridge, filling, or denture must take intoaccount that the biting force of an average human has been estimated to be approximately 1000 lbs. per square millimeter. In addition, the material used must stand up to a wet, warm, and acidic environment.

For all kinds of reasons, from psychological to financial, it's important to realize that the right dental solutions can restore oral health for a lifetime. Many of the restorative treatments a dentist provides can boast great longevity. It is not unheard of for a dental restoration (crown, bridge, and so forth) to last more than 20 years. In fact, I just had a crown on my lower molar replaced after 29 years. Not bad for a replacement part.

Your Health and Happiness is at Stake

I have noticed that when individuals allow the domino effect of dental disease to occur and their over all oral health drastically declines, they may finally overcome the fear of going to the dentist. But they still avoid the issue because they have a new problem. The state of their oral health is embarrassing and they fear being humiliated by a dentist because they have ignored their oral health and along with decay and structural problems, their teeth look bad, too.

Let me assure you that before being allowed the privilege of practicing, dental education involves treating many patients with a variety of oral health problems. In addition, dentists take an oath at the dental school graduation ceremony. Like the Hippocratic oath doctors take, the dentists' oath affirms dedication to service and requires our commitment to uphold oral healthcare among our patients.

Dentists and hygienists are there to help you, and if these individuals are practicing their professions honorably and with compassion, they will never laugh or belittle a patient for poor oral health. In most cases, new patients in this situation will be surprised by the understanding attitude of the dentist and staff. Most dentists will go out of their way to make sure these particular patients understand the treatment plan and how it is best implemented.

In my seventeen years in dentistry, I have seen hundreds of patients whose oral health had deteriorated. Many of them were executives of large companies, lawyers, physicians, and many other people who hold responsible jobs and who play an active role in the community. These patients learned to feel comfortable in seeking better oral health care. In return, they were treated with respect and admiration for overcoming the self-imposed embarrassment of their oral health status.

That said, let's look at the kind of "replacement" dentistry that is available today. These techniques are used in a variety of situations and they can help you feel better—and look your best, too.

Chapter Twelve

• • •

"Form and Function" in Your Mouth

Much of today's dentistry involves not only restoring function, but also keeping the "form." In this context, I mean the way the mouth looks. For example, I may perform root canal treatment and place a crown, procedures which address "function." If I place a crown designed to match the look of the other teeth, then I've crossed a theoretical line and am restoring "form," or put another way, the patient and I have made a "cosmetic" decision. These decisions are routine in dental practice today, largely because the goal for most individuals is to retain the teeth and the natural smile.

Avoiding the Last Resort

Although tooth extraction is almost always a safe procedure, in today's dentistry it is considered a "last resort" choice. A generation ago, about 60 percent of men and women over age 65 had lost all their natural teeth. However, by the mid-1980s, that percentage had dropped to 41 percent. It continues to decline, and many factors are involved in this change, the most important of which involve the considerable advances in dentistry. These advances allow us to work with patients to repair and restore existing teeth and in essence, maintain the ability to chew their food in a normal manner, and equally important, keep a natural smile. Even when a tooth has been extracted, we have ways to "fill in the empty space," so to speak.

Of course, the benefits of restorative dentistry are not only for the elderly. The techniques are available to everyone. For example, individuals of any age may require a dental bridge or dental implants to "fill in the empty space" created by removing a tooth. Here is a quick reference guide to these common dental procedures:

Dental Bridge: This is a prosthetic appliance that is permanently cemented to the teeth adjacent to the empty space created from a tooth extraction. These teeth are reduced so the bridge can properly fit in a patient's mouth. The *pontic* is a term used to describe the tooth that actually fills the empty space and is part of the bridge that is cemented to the adjacent teeth. (See Figure 6)

Advantages:
1. Replaces missing tooth or teeth space.
2. Can function in a patient for many years.
3. Provides good aesthetics.
4. Can usually be completed in 2-3 visits, depending

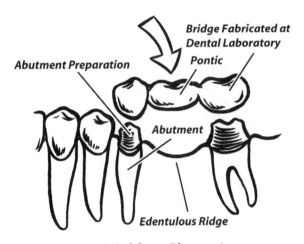

Abutment Preparation

Bridge Fabricated at Dental Laboratory

Pontic

Abutment

Edentulous Ridge

A Bridge - Figure 6.

on the difficulty of the particular case.

Disadvantages:

1. Need to reduce adjacent teeth, and that involves the risk of causing discomfort in these teeth, hence the possibility that root canal treatment will be needed.

2. Can be difficult to properly clean, so special oral hygiene supplies may be needed.

3. Cost will be more as compared to a removable denture.

4. Involves a dental laboratory to fabricate the bridge; therefore, a patient will need to wear a temporary bridge for a few weeks prior to insertion of the permanent bridge.

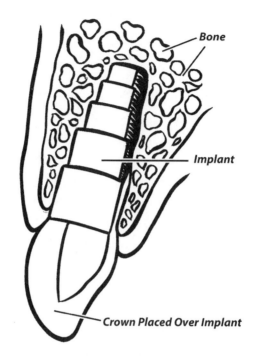

Bone

Implant

Crown Placed Over Implant

An Implant - Figure 7.

Dental Implants: A prosthetic device made out of titanium metal, the implant is placed within the upper or lower jaw to help support a crown, bridge, or denture. An implant is biocompatible with the body and is placed in the space created by the extracted tooth. (See Figure 7)

Advantages:

1. Can replace missing teeth without using adjacent teeth.

2. Can be used to support and retain dentures, espe-

cially lower dentures, because bone loss can occur from missing teeth.

3. Can function for many years.

Disadvantages:

1. Although implants can have what is called an "immediate" load (the ability to place a temporary crown or denture on the implant right after the dentist places it in the mouth) placed upon them, it can take up to a year for the bone to fill in around the implant in order to permanently stabilize it.

2. Because it can take up to a year for the bone to fill in around an implant, the final restoration (crown or denture) can not be placed until that time.

3. Implant placement into the jaw can be limited by anatomical considerations, i.e., the maxillary sinus of the upper jaw.

4. Implants can clinically fail because the bone does not properly integrate into the implant fixture.

5. Cost can be more as compared to a fixed bridge or removable denture.

Chapter Thirteen

• • •

AVOIDING THE DAILY GRIND

Do you grind your teeth at night? Do you clench your jaw when you're wide-awake or when you're asleep? Teeth grinding or jaw clenching can be triggered for physiological reasons or by external factors such as stress. Physiological grinding can occur when you are lying on your back during sleep. When your lower jaw drops slightly back and the back teeth touch, that can trigger a grinding action.

Most people are familiar with stress and encounter some type of stress on a regular basis. Most of us grind or clench as a response to stress, and this action can become so habitual that we barely notice that we're doing it. However, you may become aware of the muscle tension in your face and temple region. The next time you feel facial muscle tension, quickly focus on your teeth. A better than 90 percent chance exists that you are clenching your teeth. If you become conscious of this clenching action, you can catch yourself "in the act," and after unclenching your teeth you should immediately feel relaxation in your facial muscles and the temporomandibular joint-the "jaw joint."

I often catch myself clenching my teeth as a response to stress. When this happens, I try to focus on the cause of the stress rather than on considering only its effects. I also remind myself that the winner of the rat race is still a rat! So, no matter what else you do to prevent teeth grinding and clenching, focus on the concept of stress and learn as much as you can about stress management. Realize, too, that grinding and clenching are *symptoms* of stress, and if you deal with the cause, the symptoms will subside.

A Problem Too Important to Overlook

Teeth grinding and clenching can cause the tooth enamel to wear. If the enamel wears to a point that the *dentin* (the semi-hard tissue under the enamel) begins to show, the tooth may start to become sensitive. Also, wearing the surfaces of teeth can cause bad *occlusion* (the term we use to describe the way our teeth come together when we bite down). As the bite begins to change, you could begin to experience muscle and jaw joint ache, headaches, and tooth mobility or fractures.

Treating the Problem

In addition to managing stress, treatment for grinding your teeth is as follows:

First, the dentist evaluates your bite and checks

for "high spots" in the bite. These spots indicate that your teeth are in contact in one region of the mouth before another. The goal is to have balanced occlusion, which is general light contact of all teeth when you bite down.

Secondly, once the occlusion is adjusted, which is usually completed without any local anesthetic, a mouth guard is fabricated. The mouth guard is a plastic or rubber mold of your teeth and is worn primarily at night. The mouth guard keeps the teeth apart to prevent the physiological tooth grinding response, thus preventing the wear on the teeth.

Typically, the mouth guard should last 6-12 months before being replaced. However, I recall a patient that I treated when I had my general dentistry practice. He came in every Friday to have his mouth guard replaced because the wear and tear on it could be likened to being run over by a Mack truck. So, each Friday, I would reiterate all the causes of grinding and clenching, and I'd ask him if he had any stress in his life that could account for this extensive tooth and jaw action. His answer was always the same: "Just the usual life battles, Doc."

These weekly patient visits went on for months, but one day he showed up in my office with the mouth guard perfectly intact. I asked him why he hadn't been using his mouth guard. He said he had been wearing it every night, but that his divorce was finally complete, he quit his miserable job, and was moving to Arizona to start a new career! So much for the "usual life battles!"

Without question, educating yourself about stress is the first "line of defense" against tooth grinding and clenching. We all need ways to manage stress, and we must seek help if we can't figure it out for ourselves. Help may come in the form of an exercise program, physical therapy, and/or professional counseling. Perhaps the company you work for offers stress management seminars. If so, sign up for one now. Or, go to the library or bookstore and get some books about stress. You'll be doing your teeth a big favor.

Chapter Fourteen

• • •

KID POWER

When it comes to our children we may have chosen a pediatrician before they are even born, but then we take them to a general dentist who treats adults—perhaps the same dentist who has treated you for years. In reality, it is important to find pediatric dental care for your child. Pediatric dentists have spent at least two years after dental school training solely in children's dentistry. These individuals have the clinical ability plus the patient management skills to make a visit to the dentist a very positive experience for your child.

As a dentist and a parent I appreciate the patient management skills of a pediatric dentist. I remember taking my youngest daughter, Jamie, for her first visit to our pediatric dentist when she turned two. As she was escorted by the dental assistant into the treatment room, the tears were running down her face. I knew I had to be the parent with the breaking heart that was requested to stay in the waiting room rather than the dentist who would go with her into the treatment area. But, after seeing the dentist, she came out into the waiting room literally skipping and was all smiles. In fact, to this day, at nine years old, she not only does not fear a trip to the dentist, but when she saw her pediatric dentist in a restaurant one evening, she ran over to his table and gave him a big hug and a kiss!

The pediatric dental office provides an environment that is less intimidating than an adult dental office. This pediatric environment is usually similar to a pediatrician's office. Parents should consider seeking professional oral health care for their children when they are about age two. If you don't know a pediatric dentist in your area, ask a friend or relative or your own dentist for a referral.

When your children reach their early teens, you can consider switching them to an adult dentist. However, as is sometimes the case with pediatricians, it is not uncommon for children to see their pediatric dentist until they finish high school. When you place your children in the care of a pediatric dentist they will grow up without fearing the dentist, and beyond that, they will understand that oral health care is as important as their general health care.

Frequently Asked Questions About Children's Oral Health

1. *How many baby (primary) teeth do children develop?*

Children have 20 primary teeth. They do not have bicuspids or third molars (wisdom teeth). Unlike adult (permanent) teeth that are numbered 1-32, children's teeth are labeled with upper case letters, A through T. A is the patient's upper right second molar and the letters continue to J, which is the patient's upper left second molar. The lower left second molar is K and continues to the lower right second molar T. (See Figure 8)

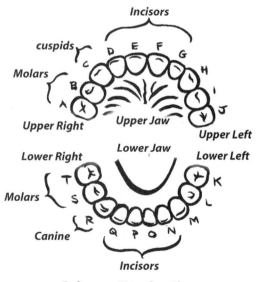

Primary Teeth - Figure 8.

2. *Can using a baby bottle cause tooth decay?*

   The actual bottle is not the cause of the tooth decay, but rather the sugar that is contained in milk (store bought, formula, and mother's milk), juice, or presweetened drinks that are placed in a bottle. When a baby's teeth have prolonged exposure (hours at a time of continuous contact of the teeth with the sugar) to a bottle, the teeth are prone to decay. A common term for this type of decay is baby bottle caries.

3. *What does a pediatric dentist do to help prevent decay in my child's teeth?*

   One of the most important steps in early prevention of tooth decay is proper patient education on brushing, flossing, and nutritional concerns (i.e., limiting sweets). The pediatric dentist may also recommend tooth sealants. This is a type of bonding agent that is placed on the surface of posterior teeth to fill in the small crevices in teeth that can harbor the bacteria that promote tooth decay. This is done without local anesthetic. The dentist also makes sure that the child receives fluoride in their water, toothpaste, or through fluoride treatments in the office. Lastly, the pediatric dentist usually places your child on six-month recall in order to prevent dental disease or catch it at an early stage. When caught early, treatment is less invasive or complex, thus making for a happier child.

4. *Can my child get gum disease?*

Yes, but not to the same extent as seen in adults. Children can get gum irritation and juvenile periodontitis (the child's form of adult gum disease, usually associated with Down's syndrome and genetic diseases). Primary teeth (baby teeth) have natural space between them called "embrasures" that allow food to pass through without getting trapped and causing gum disease. The gum can become inflamed but with oral hygiene help from the parents and the natural immune response from the child, there is very minimal chance of bone and tooth loss due to gum disease. All permanent teeth erupt by the late teens, which allows plenty of time for your child to become educated about oral health and physically coordinated enough to properly brush and floss their teeth. Good oral hygiene, along with natural immune response, generally means that gum disease remains minimal up to the late teens and twenties.

Braces are the New Fashion Statement Among Kids

Times have changed. When I was growing up, wearing braces left a kid vulnerable to being called names. But today, braces are very much in style. My own kids are hoping their teeth will be crooked enough to get braces. In fact, my oldest daughter,

Allie, has already decided what color bands she'd like to have.

The American Association of Orthodontists recommends that children be evaluated by an orthodontist at the age of 7. Although actual orthodontic treatment does not usually occur until the child is between 11-13 years of age, evaluation of the teeth and jaw development at 7 years old allows for early intervention of treatment if necessary.

Before starting any type of treatment, the orthodontist will make tooth records and mouth models, along with taking photos and x-rays of the face and teeth. The orthodontist does a thorough evaluation in order to decide if and when any treatment is necessary. Next, the parents, the child, and the orthodontist will have a discussion about treatment options and the projected length of treatment. Although the length of time your child wears braces can vary greatly, the average length of treatment is two years. After the completion of orthodontic treatment, it is not uncommon for the child to wear a retainer (fixed or removable) to prevent the teeth from moving back into their pretreatment position. The retainer is usually worn for two years after treatment, but ideally the orthodontist will encourage the child to wear it, even on a limited basis, for longer than that.

"Don't Panic Mom, But I Hit My Front Tooth!"

One of a parent's worst nightmares is when their child comes home with a fractured, partially displaced, or *avulsed* (totally out of the socket) tooth. Many parents are comfortable treating minor medical emergencies like cuts and bruises, but when it comes to handling trauma of the permanent teeth, they develop a total "brain freeze" in providing first-aid for teeth. This is primarily due to lack of information about what to do.

First, don't panic! Then, if the tooth was knocked out of the mouth, make sure the tooth does not dry out. Place the tooth in milk or saliva (if the child is able they can spit into a cup). Next, contact your child's dentist and try to get in as soon as possible, ideally within an hour of the tooth trauma.

If the tooth is totally out the socket, the dentist will place the tooth back in to the mouth and into its normal position. Then the dentist splints the tooth to the adjacent teeth with monofilament (fishing line type material), an arched wire (usually made of nickel titanium metal), or with a bonding material to help support it. He or she will do a full examination of the boney structures of the face to check for fractures, exam the soft tissue (face, lips and gum tissue) for cuts and check the other teeth to make sure they were not injured. The dentist may prescribe antibiotics, pain medications, and an antiseptic mouth rinse. In addition, they may tell the parents to find out (within the next 48 hours) the date of the child's last tetanus shot. The pediatrician will be able to advise the parents if another shot is needed.

The splint will be kept in place for about 7-10 days. During this time, it is important for the child not to bite on the splint and to maintain good home oral hygiene.

After the splint is removed the vitality (a test to determine if the nerve and blood supply in the tooth is alive) of a tooth is tested by placing a cold substance on it or by testing it with what is called an electric pulp tester. This instrument sends a faint electric charge through the tooth; if the tooth is vital, the patient will feel a "tingling" sensation in the tooth. It should be noted that the chance of a tooth regenerating its blood and nerve supply after being out of the socket is minimal. If the tooth does regenerate its nerve and blood supply, the child will be seen frequently over the course of weeks and months in order to continually check to see if the tooth remains vital. Usually, if the tooth stays vital up to a year, the prognosis of the tooth remaining vital is favorable. The dentist will restore the tooth if needed, in order to provide good aesthetics for the patient.

If the tooth is diagnosed as necrotic, meaning that the blood and nerve supply has died, after the splint has been removed, the dentist will first determine through x-ray examination if the root is fully developed. If it's not fully developed, then root canal treatment is initiated and medication (usually calcium hydroxide) is placed in the tooth to help the root end to continue to develop. A root can develop even though it is dead. (Is Mother Nature wonderful or what?) After the root develops, which usually takes 6-12 months, the root canal procedure can be completed by filling the root canal space with gutta-percha and sealer and then the tooth is restored. The child will be seen frequently for at least a year so the tooth can be monitored.

If the root is diagnosed as necrotic but the root is fully formed, the dentist will start root canal treatment, which involves placing medication (calcium hydroxide) into the tooth. The medication treatment is repeated every few months for up to a year. This medication is used in order to help prevent *resorption*, meaning that the body's immune system cannot eat away at the root in response to the trauma, and *ankylosis* (the fusion of the bone in the tooth socket to the actual tooth) of the root, or bone loss around the tooth.

After 6-12 months of medication treatment, the tooth is evaluated. The dentist will examine the tooth to determine if it appears healthy and find out if the child is experiencing any pain. If an x-ray reveals no signs of root *resorption, ankylosis,* or excessive bone loss, the dentist will complete the root canal treatment and restore the tooth. The patient will be placed on recall and followed for a year or so.

If for some reason the traumatized tooth begins to

be painful or shows swelling or x-rays show signs of *resorption, ankylosis*, or bone loss, then the dentist may offer other treatment options. These include root canal surgery to treat the defect in the root, or extraction and replacement with an implant or bridge.

In cases in which a tooth is chipped or fractured in an accident, it is still important to see the dentist right away. In these cases, too, dentists do a full examination of the bones of the face to check for any fractures. They also examine soft tissue (face, lips and gums) for cuts and test the teeth for vitality. If the tooth in question tests normal, that is, it responds to cold or the electric pulp test, then cosmetic treatment may be indicated. However, the child will need frequent evaluation for up to a year. If the tooth should become necrotic, then a root canal is the treatment of choice.

In cases when the tooth is chipped or fractured and the actual root nerve and blood supply is visible, a couple of treatment options are available, depending on the tooth's vitality status. If the tooth responds to cold but the sensation does not linger beyond five seconds, then the nerve is partially removed and medication (calcium hydroxide or mineral trioxide aggregate) is placed over the remaining nerve. Then the tooth is restored and the patient is placed on recall. If the tooth responds to cold beyond five seconds, then a root canal treatment is performed because this is a sign that the nerve is inflamed to a point that it cannot heal itself. The tooth will be restored after the root canal treatment, and the patient placed on recall for further re-evaluation.

Trauma to Primary (Baby) Teeth

When a child has an accident that involves a primary tooth, the dentist is not going to recommend placing it back in the mouth if the tooth is avulsed or displaced within the socket. If the tooth involved remains fixed in the socket, there is a good chance that in time the tooth will become discolored, which is a sign that blood is being trapped in the tooth. (I'm personally familiar with this scenario.) In addition, the tooth may start to resorb or the root canal space may become calcificied. The dentist will continue to monitor the tooth to see if these conditions are developing. If the tooth starts to resorb early then it may be extracted; if it calcifies, it usually is kept in the mouth until it naturally resorbs. The bottom line is the dentist will need to continually evaluate if the trauma to your child's primary tooth has an effect on the development of the permanent tooth below it. This evaluation is done through clinical and radiographic examinations.

Tips to melt away the dental trauma "brain freeze":
1. If there is any bleeding from the soft tissue of the face, lips or gums, gently clean the area with a

moistened cloth. If the bleeding continues, place an ice pack wrapped in a cloth over the area and apply pressure.

2. Call your child's dentist immediately!
3. Remember, dental trauma can be an inexact science. The dentist can do the most up-to-date treatment for your child's tooth, but over time the tooth may still need further treatment, including extraction. It is not uncommon to see effects from dental injuries many years later as an adult. For example, we can see calcification of the root canal, bone loss around the tooth, root resorption or ankylosis occurring many years after a traumatic incident to a tooth.
4. Dental injuries to your child never seem to happen at an opportune time. There always seems to be an upcoming important family event—a wedding or a Bar Mitzvah or a graduation—when a perfect smile is required! Take comfort and realize that modern dentistry offers the best possibilities to give your child a great smile!

The Best Defense is Having One

Over 80 percent of dental trauma involves the upper front teeth (maxillary central incisors) followed by the teeth immediately adjacent called the maxillary lateral incisors. The lower front teeth (mandibular central incisors) come in a close second for traumatic injuries, along with the teeth adjacent (the mandibular lateral incisors).

The best prevention is making sure that your child is properly protected to ensure safety during their physical activity. Unfortunately, parents often worry about padding and protection for the body and head and do not put as much stock in protecting the mouth. However, a mouth guard or facemask, depending on the specific activity, should be included in the standard equipment for physical endeavor. Fortunately, a mouth guard can be made by a dentist or bought at a store and made at home. The dentist will make a model of your child's teeth to create the mouth guard. A mouth guard bought at a sporting good store can be customized for your child's mouth by softening it in warm water.

Chapter Fifteen

• • •

BUILDING BONDS—SORT OF

Cosmetic concerns are almost universal today. It's a rare person who does not want to have a pleasant smile, part of which depends on attractive teeth. As we grow older, our teeth may show some wear and tear in the form of stains and discoloration, and physical damage such as cracks and chips. At some point, you may ask what can be done to improve the appearance of your teeth without necessarily moving them around (orthodontics) or giving them completely new "covers" (crowns). Most general dentists offer the following procedures:

Bleaching (or whitening): You may love your morning coffee or tea, but as you probably know, these substances may stain your teeth. In addition, smoking leaves telltale stains, and the teeth of a smoker who does not receive regular dental cleanings may become yellow-brown. In addition, certain antibiotics, like tetracycline, may discolor the teeth. This occurs if the antibiotic was given during the time when the permanent teeth were first developing prior to eruption. Finally, the teeth may become discolored through the normal aging process. Tooth bleaching may help restore the color of the teeth, but the procedure should be done only on healthy teeth. In other words, it does no good to try to "bleach" the discoloration that is caused by decay or a dead nerve or worn away fillings. You can't bleach away the need for dental treatment.

Tooth bleaching can be done in the dental office, using a solution or gel containing hydrogen peroxide or carbamide peroxide. This in-office procedure is done on teeth that have been cleaned, meaning that all plaque and surface stains are removed. This type of bleaching may require several office visits. Depending on the whitening system that a dentist may use, the gel or solution is placed in a custom-made mouth tray or applied by painting the gel directly on the teeth and then activating it with a high-powered light. If a custom tray is used, it involves creating a plaster mold of your teeth and a mouthpiece—similar to a tray—is made to match that mold. The bleaching solution is put into tray, and you wear the mouthpiece for several hours a day over a period of about two weeks.

When the gel is directly applied to your teeth and activated with a light, you don't need to use a whitening system at home. However, you may need to see the dentist for more than one treatment, depending on the actual shade of white that you are trying to achieve.

Most people are pleased with either type of

whitening treatment results, but a few side effects can be expected. For example, temporary gum irritation and tooth sensitivity may occur. In addition, bleaching may not be uniform and not all stains may bleach out. Some people complain of a sore jaw from wearing the mouthpiece. However, despite these concerns, tooth bleaching is becoming increasingly popular.

You may have seen at-home bleaching kits advertised on television. In general, these whitening kits contain the same solution or gel as stated above, (hydrogen peroxide or carbamide peroxide) but in lesser concentration than a dentist uses. The patient will either brush the material on their teeth or place a "whitening strip" across their front teeth. It may take multiple uses to see any cosmetic effects. Although you may see some results, it is not the same as a dentist treating and monitoring the progression of tooth lightening change.

Bonding: This cosmetic treatment addresses cracks and chips and can rebuild the edges of teeth and re-contour a tooth. It can also be used over discoloration of a tooth. Bonding material is a composite resin; it is applied to a tooth that has been treated with a mild acidic solution that allows the "bond" to form. After the bonding material is placed on the tooth, the dentist uses a special light that activates the material, allowing it to set. On occasion, bonding may irritate the gum if it is applied close to the gum line. The composite material may stain or crack over time and need to be replaced. Composite resin can also be used to fill cavities when cosmetic considerations are a concern.

The advantage of using composite resin as a bonding material is that the dentist can apply it to a tooth and you can see an immediate change in its appearance. It does not involve taking impressions (mouth moldings) that are sent out to a dental laboratory for fabrication. In addition, if you should re-stain or chip the composite filling, a dentist can easily repair it. Bonds usually last an average of 5 to 15 years, depending on the placement of the tooth and the extent of the bonding.

Veneers: Like bonding, this technique involves repairing the tooth by restoring its shape and color. Veneers involve cementing customized pieces of porcelain or composite over the tooth in order to change its appearance. The procedure involves the possible reduction of a tooth's front surface and then taking a dental impression. The impression is sent to a dental lab where it is used as a model. Then, the porcelain or composite veneer is fabricated on the model. After the dentist receives the veneer back from the lab, he or she will bond it to the tooth surface.

Porcelain is preferred over resin because it does not stain or scratch easily. But a composite resin veneer can be repaired without having to send it back to the dental lab. Porcelain or composite veneers can be shaped to change the appearance of a tooth and even the placement of the teeth, thus making irregularly spaced teeth appear more evenly spaced.

Veneers can chip or crack over time, and generally last five years or so, after which they need to be replaced. Like dental bonds, they can cause irritation along the gum line.

Asking the Right Questions

Cosmetic dentistry is not exactly a new field, but its techniques have become available to more people. In addition, for many people, an attractive smile is viewed as a professional necessity, not to mention important on a personal level. However, it is as important to be an informed patient when you "shop" for these cosmetic procedures as it is when you seek any other dental care. When you talk to your dentist (or a new dentist) about the possibility of cosmetic dental work, be sure to probe for information. I recommend the following questions:

- Is the treatment (any cosmetic procedure) the latest technique? Or, is there an older, more reliable method the dentist uses? (While you want up-to-date care, the "latest" method may not be an improvement on the old techniques and it may not have stood the test of time.)
- Is special training required? Any dentist should be willing to discuss his or her training in a specific technique. If the dentist is not well-trained, you

should expect to be referred to someone who is.

- Are other techniques available that might achieve the same result?
- What are the *possible* complications or side effects? At what frequency do they occur?
- What should the result be?
- How often will I need the treatment repeated?
- Will I need local anesthetic in order to perform the cosmetic treatment?

Cosmetic dentistry is an exciting field, and without question, these techniques have helped many people overcome self-consciousness and have increased self-confidence. Gather information and ask the right questions, and you are likely to feel good about your decision.

A Nickel's Worth of Advice for Free

The media have created a false impression about cosmetic dentistry. Many of my patients who have consulted with me about cosmetic treatment want their teeth to be "movie star" or "super-model white." However, I tell them to be aware that photos of fashion models and movie stars have been airbrushed to perfection, or veneers have been placed and have been over-whitened for the cameras.

In reality, nature has given very few people perfectly white teeth. And most people have some form of yellow or brownish staining on their teeth caused by everyday use. So when receiving cosmetic tooth treatment, keep your expectations of Hollywood in check. Believe me, very white teeth look very unnatural.

Cosmetic Dentistry Poster Child

Some people are born into greatness; others have it thrust upon them, while still others realize at a very young age they are probably going to become dentists. I fall into the latter category. At the age of two I fell on the sidewalk and hit my front tooth. Within a month it turned black, and remained that way until my permanent tooth erupted and allowed the cosmetically displeasing baby tooth to fall out. You have to remember that in those days pediatric cosmetic dentistry involved telling the parents that it's okay for your child to look like that because he's still a kid.

After my brand spanking new front tooth had erupted, I was horsing around with my older brother one day when I landed my new front tooth into the back of his head. The trauma caused the tooth to push forward out of the socket. My family dentist pushed it back into place, but in time, the tooth ended up chipped and discolored. Over the next few years I had the tooth bleached and bonded for aesthetic reasons. During this time in my youth, my crooked teeth would never see braces because I fought adamantly against them. In my mind, the names—brace-face, wire-mouth, and so forth—the other kids would call me were worse than not having perfectly straight teeth.

Later in my adult life, with the advent of Starbucks® coffee and tea, my teeth began to stain and I ended up having cosmetic dental treatment again. Bonding was performed to help give my front teeth a more straightened appearance and bleaching helped to lighten up and eliminate the staining. I am happy to report that I have reduced my coffee and tea intake and am very satisfied with my own smile. Most importantly, the current cosmetic dental experience was pleasant and actually required little if any local anesthesia. Most of the treatment was completed in one visit, because there was no dental lab work involved.

Finally Getting it Straight as an Adult

The person who coined the phrase "hindsight is 20/20" must have been an adult who never got braces as a kid for one reason or another. Looking back, I regret being a rebellious kid who went against my parents when it came to getting braces. Today, many adults go through orthodontic treatment. There used to be a myth that people past their late teens would have difficulty with orthodontic treatment. However, tooth movement is possible at any age.

If you are interested in straightening your teeth,

I recommend that you seek treatment from an orthodontist because these individuals have the skill level to provide the right treatment plan. Orthodontists spend two to three years beyond dental school learning to treat teeth that are out of alignment.

Some newer methods of orthodontic treatment for adults do not even involve using actual braces. In some cases, a patient can wear a series of clear mouth appliances that will gradually rotate and move teeth into the proper position. The only real drawback to adult orthodontic treatment is the timeframe, which can vary from a few months to a period of years. In addition, it is not uncommon for teeth that have been repositioned to revert back, thus making it necessary for the patient to wear a fixed or removable retainer to help prevent tooth movement.

Since adult orthodontic patients have stopped growing, there can be limitations to how much orthodontic treatment alone can correct the positioning of teeth. Sometimes jaw surgery or tooth extraction needs to be done in conjunction with braces to properly correct a patient's bite and cosmetic problems.

Chapter Sixteen

• • •

KICKING FEAR IN THE REAR

Dental anxiety, fear and/or phobia are not confined to individuals. It is pervasive in our society, and it is "politically correct" to be afraid of the dentist. I hope that the information presented in this book has alleviated at least some of your fear and negative reactions to dentistry.

Empowerment Fights Back At Fear

Empowering yourself with information about the unknown is important for overcoming any fear. A few years ago (prior to 9/11/01), I developed a fear of flying. This was a serious issue because I was lecturing in the U.S. and abroad, so I flew thousands of miles each year. I began to feel fear and anxiety every time I arrived at the airport. When my fear was close to the point at which I seriously considered not scheduling any more lecture dates so that I could stop flying, I knew it was time to get help. I went on-line and gathered information on various Web sites that led me to a few books that dealt with fear of flying.

This information helped me feel better about flying.

First, I learned how planes operate and then I read about some "tricks" that would help me with my anxiety during take-off and landing. One of my biggest problems was overcoming the loss of control I felt while flying. I took comfort in knowing that literally millions of other people shared this same fear. Unfortunately, we need to compromise when dealing with the control issue because the Federal Aviation Administration is not going let "air phobics" take on the role of pilot just to gain a sense of control. The larger point is that information helped me overcome my fear of flying. Educating myself *empowered* me.

Fortunately, dental phobics have an advantage over flying phobics because they *can* take some steps to gain a control over their environment, and loss of control is a primary fear among dental phobics. Even the physical position you're in while in the chair (lying back) and the proximity required for the dentist to work in the mouth can send up a lot of red flags for patients. Psychologists tell us that on average, we need two to three feet of personal space around us. Even the television show, *Seinfeld*, used this premise in an episode. You may remember it. Elaine's friend was nicknamed "the close talker" because he always got right in the person's face when he talked. The show was funny because we all recognize the need for personal space and we may back away when we perceive that someone is "invading" it. Dentists and hygienists must cross the invisible barrier in order to perform the work required, whether that's an examination, cleaning, or working on an individual tooth. It's easy to understand how this increases fear in a dental patient in general and dental phobics in particular.

Some dentists provide a therapeutic eye cover that not only blocks the view of the dentist's (or hygienist's) face, but also soothes the eye region, much like you would experience at a spa. In addition, dentists wear advanced magnification glasses (called loupes) that enlarge the treatment field. This also allows them to limit their encroachment in your personal space. These steps help patients feel they are in greater control over this often unspoken need for physical distance.

In the past, dentists treated patients with their bare hands and without mouth protection. Because of the necessary proximity, dentists breathed on their patients while sticking their still wet, freshly washed hands in their patients' mouth. When I was kid, my dentist used the worst smelling soap, and then he'd breathe all over me when he examined my mouth. As I saw it, the view from the dental chair was not pretty.

Happily, times have changed. Dentists now wear gloves and a protective mask over their mouth and nose. They still wash their hands in between patients, but gloves give their hands a very neutral taste, feel, and smell. As a consumer of regular dental care, I find this a great improvement in the dental field.

Communicate, Communicate

Access to information has changed the patient-dentist relationship. The Internet alone has allowed patients to become better informed about dental procedures, but general information is no substitute for face-to-face explanations from a dentist. Most dental offices have a separate consultation room, which are like a regular business office. These rooms are often used as a more comfortable setting in which to discuss patients' treatment plans. If you harbor fear of the dentist, then you are likely to be better able to listen and ask questions about treatment when you're sitting in a regular chair in an office. The dental chair itself may trigger bad memories of earlier dental care, and it may also lead to the sense of "invasion" referred to earlier.

To further develop control in the dental chair, discuss a signal that will alert the dentist to stop the procedure immediately. You can be free to use this signal not only if you feel physical discomfort during the procedure, but for anything that may make you feel uneasy and trigger the fear.

Other Tips

Consider the following information as a plan to help overcome this dental fear:

- Get a dentist referral from a friend, co-worker, or relative. Do not blindly point to a name in the phonebook.

- Try to make an early-morning appointment. You will be fresh and will not have all day to worry about seeing the dentist. Make sure that you eat a light breakfast; this will help you better deal with the stress of being in a dental office. When you call to schedule the appointment, tell the person you speak to that you are a new patient who is trying to overcome a fear of the dentist. You need a morning appointment and adequate time to ask questions and feel comfortable. In most cases, you will be accommodated. If the scheduler shows a lack of understanding and does not courteously address your need, then call another dental office. Your request should be honored.

- Try to arrive a little early for your appointment. Besides having to fill out some forms, insurance information and health history, for example, the extra time allows you to adapt physically and mentally to the environment.

- Don't be afraid to ask the dentist questions. You may want to write down these questions or concerns; if you don't put them in writing, you may forget them once you're actually there. Unless your visit involves an acute problem that is causing pain, have only an examination and x-rays at the first visit. This will eliminate the fear involved with drills and fillings.

- If possible, discuss a treatment plan on the same day, but realize that some dentists schedule an additional appointment to discuss the recommended plan. In most cases, the first recommended treatment is having your teeth cleaned by the hygienist.

- If any further treatment such as filling a cavity or cosmetic work is needed, then you will schedule subsequent appointments. Most dental treatment can be completed in one visit. When laboratory work is required, such as fabricating a crown or a denture, you will need a second appointment.

Once your dentist tells you that your mouth is in good shape, the office will recommend that you be placed on six-month recall, which means that every six months you will return for a teeth cleaning and oral examination. Since it takes six months for a cavity to first appear, this interval greatly increases your chances for treating decay in its early stage and catching any gum disease or oral pathology early, too. Regular care is reassuring because your dental appointments likely will be routine and involve minimal treatment. Your anxiety, fear, or phobia about dentistry is likely to fade away, because you will know exactly what to expect.

Gasoline on the Fire

As an aside, for the person who fears going to the dentist, the only motivating factor is pain! Unfortunately, this is the worst possible scenario for a dental phobic. Pain caused by dental problems can cause sleep disturbance, loss of appetite, and a constant need for pain medication. Usually, the pain becomes so bad that the person finally calls a dentist—and does not hang up the phone when someone answers!

Unfortunately, the dental office immediately stirs up the bad memories that may have caused the phobia. When you combine a toothache with lack of sleep and poor diet with sitting in a dental chair, it is like pouring gasoline on a fire. This soon causes panic to kick in. I've seen this happen. The patient's heart begins racing, and he or she may begin sweating and gripping the arms of the dental chair.

As an endodontist, I see this type of patient on a daily basis, and I know for sure that patients who are in pain are irritable and have a very short attention span. They have a difficult time listening when I attempt to explain the diagnosis and proper dental treatment. All they want is for the pain to go away. What has always amazed me is when these patients are phoned that evening to see how they are doing after their dental treatment, they reveal dramatically different personalities. With their pain gone, they become their own happy selves again. I can't stress the importance of starting down the path to better oral health by seeing a dentist before you develop tooth pain.

Remember that dentistry today is a highly technological field that can perform its numerous procedures without causing great pain. Twenty-first century dentistry is light years away from what it was even 10-15 years ago. So re-examine your old beliefs about dentistry, because the importance of your oral health can't be overestimated. Optimal oral health helps you eat and speak better—and look better, too. As I've said before, a healthy and cosmetically pleasing smile enhances self-esteem, and improving a smile is one of the most dramatic cosmetic procedures done in all of medicine.

An Important Commitment

Oral health care can be accomplished in as little as two dentist visits per year. This is a very minimal time commitment to assure good oral health over a lifetime.

In *The Tipping Point*, author Malcolm Gladwell writes about how certain *small* events (termed tipping points) can cause a larger epidemic-type change within a population. Gladwell writes: "Look at the world around you. It may seem like an immovable, implacable place. It is not. With the slightest push—in just the right place—it can be tipped." Perhaps the information presented here can help "tip" the way dentistry is viewed by those who have anxiety and fear about dentists and dentistry. I certainly hope that what I have provided here will cause a significant change in the way you think and feel about your oral health care!

• • •

ABOUT THE AUTHOR

Dr. James K. Bahcall is an Assistant Professor and Chairman of the Department of Surgical Sciences at Marquette University School of Dentistry, Milwaukee, Wisconsin. He also is the Director of the Postgraduate Endodontic Residency Program at Marquette. He received his BS degree from the University of Wisconsin, his DMD degree from Tufts University School of Dental Medicine and an MS degree and certificate in Endodontics from Marquette University School of Dentistry. Dr. Bahcall is a Diplomate of the American Board of Endodontics and a Fellow in The International College of Dentists. He pioneered and is a leading authority on fiber optic and endoscopic visualization in the field of endodontics. Dr. Bahcall has been the recipient of outstanding teaching awards and has published numerous scientific articles, as well as written chapters for endodontic textbooks. He lectures on endodontics both nationally and internationally. Dr. Bahcall has been married to his wife, Amy, for 12 years, and has two children: Alexis, 11 and Jamie, 9. They reside in Chicago.

APPENDIX

American Dental Association
211 East Chicago Ave.
Chicago, IL 60611-2678
Phone: 1-312-440-2500
www.ada.org

American Association of Endodontists
211 East Chicago Ave.
Suite 1100
Chicago, IL 60611-2637
Phone: 1-800-872-3636
www.aae.org

American Association of Oral and Maxillofacial
Surgeons
9700 W. Bryn Mawr Ave.
Rosemont, IL 60018-5701
Phone: 1-847-678-6200
www.aaoms.org

American Association of Public Health Dentistry
Suite 400B
1224 Centre West
Springfield, IL 62704
Phone: 1-217-391-0218
www.aaphd.org

American Academy of Pediatric Dentistry
211 East Chicago Ave.
Suite 700
Chicago, IL 60611-2663
Phone: 1-312-337-2169
www.aapd.org

American Academy of Periodontology
737 North Michigan Ave.
Suite 800
Chicago, IL 60611-2615
Phone: 1-312-787-5518
www.perio.org

American College of Prosthodontists
211 East Chicago Ave.
Suite 1100
Chicago, IL 60611-2637
Phone: 1-312-573-1260
www.prosthodontics.org

American Academy of Oral and Maxillofacial
Pathology
710 E. Ogden Ave.
Suite 600
Naperville, IL 60563-8602
Phone: 1-888-552-2667
www.aaomp.org

American Academy of Oral and Maxillofacial
Radiology
P.O. Box 1010
Evan, GA 30809-1010
Phone: 1-706-721-2607
www.aaomr.org

GLOSSARY OF COMMON DENTAL TERMS

Amalgam: A silver filling material that is a mixture of different metals.

Anesthesia: The loss of feeling or pain sensation.

Antibiotic Prophylaxis: The use of antibiotics to protect against infection.

Bridge: Porcelain fused to metal or all metal fabricated teeth that replace a missing tooth or teeth.

Calculus: Dental plaque that hardens due to contact with saliva.

Cavity: Tooth decay. The dental jargon for cavity is *caries.*

Cementum: The mineralized tissue that covers a tooth root's outer surface.

Crown: Porcelain fused to metal or an all metal fabricated tooth that covers the existing tooth's crown portion.

Composite filling: A tooth-colored filling that is made of a resin material.

D.D.S.: Doctor of Dental Surgery.

Decay: The erosion of a tooth or root surface due to bacteria.

Dentin: The mineral tissue that is under the enamel and cementum tooth surface.